BROKEN
BUT NOT
DESTROYED

*Living On Purpose Daily Devotional
& Personal Journal*

PASTOR MAVIS E. MORISSEAU

Exulon Elite

Copyright © 2015 by Pastor Mavis E. Morisseau

Broken but Not Destroyed
Living On Purpose Daily Devotional & Personal Journal
by Pastor Mavis E. Morisseau

Edited by Rev. Stephanie Harley
Photographer (author photo) – Mylan Morisseau
Contributing Cover Designers – Tonya Mills & Ruthy Deal
Joseph's Coat of Many Colors Designer – Michele Vela

Printed in the United States of America.

ISBN 9781498429344

All rights reserved solely by the author. The author guarantees all contents are original and do not infringe upon the legal rights of any other person or work. No part of this book may be reproduced in any form without the permission of the author. The views expressed in this book are not necessarily those of the publisher.

Unless otherwise indicated, Scripture quotations taken from the The Holy Bible, New International Version (NIV). Copyright © 1973, 1978, 1984, 2011 by Biblica, Inc.™. Used by permission. All rights reserved.

Scripture quotations taken from the New King James Version (NKJV). Copyright © 1982 by Thomas Nelson, Inc. Used by permission. All rights reserved.

Scripture quotations taken from the King James Version (KJV) – *public domain.*

www.xulonpress.com

CONTENTS

Dedication vii
Foreword xiii
Introduction ix
Poem xi

Part I

1. Our Inner Life with God 19
2. Residue of Abuse 23
3. A Recurring Cycle 29
4. Rotten Roots 35
5. My World 40
6. My Damascus Road 47

Part II

7. The Healing Process 51
8. Pivotal Points 61
9. Finishing the Race 64
10. Exercise Patience for the Promises 68
11. Forgive Your Abusers 73
12. Restoring Trust 80
13. Fill My Cup 84
14. God Rewards Faithfulness 89
15. Spiritual Therapy for Victory 93
16. Daily Bread for Maintaining Your Deliverance (Workbook) . 95
    "Personal Development through Prayer"
    "Who Am I"
    "Never Again"
    "Affirmation of Faith and Holiness"

About the Author 121

DEDICATION

I wish to dedicate this book to my children and grandchildren; Terranie, Chavon, Jonae, Ashonta & Andre, Joseph, Samenta, Mylan, Micah, Alana, Saraiyah, TaYon, and Cheyenne who showed me my life and the choices that I made was not worth losing them to the world.

Special thanks to: Rev. Stephanie Harley, Jordan Harley, Sis. Michaelle Banks, Chelsi Banks, Dr. Mateen Diop, Ms. Wilma Hicks, Jocelyn and Marvin Porter, Edward Hardeman, John Hardeman, Elsie Cyrs, Colby Cyrs, Elder Norman Hicks, Charlene Wynn, Darlene Wynn, Marlene Wynn, Joann Minnfee, Mr. Kai Dupe, Dixon family, Ellison family, Rev. Sandy Smith, Evangelist Carolie and Tor Lenoir, Mr. and Mrs. Rounds, Rev. Kristen Simpson, Sis. Diana Pryme, Sis. Beverly Simmons, Sis. Sadiqa Pettaway, Pastor Andra Standberry, April Allen, Ms. Mary Gooden, Sis. Phyllis Jordan, Elder Delores Kingwood, Min. Wanda Hill, Yvette Glasgow, Pastor Mary Stewart, Kelly Greene, George Flagherty, Nnena Wilson, Sharon Nimmons, Onita Davis, Deacon Nathaniel Rollins, Min. Gary Washington, Elder Lisa Wilson, Bro. Howard Rollins, Sis. Renee Alexander, Dr. Russell Groves, Rev. Matthew McCoy, Pastor Rudolph McCoy, Mr. Keith Key, Minister Karen Gardner, Janice Suitte, Robin Shaw, Sharon Golden, Allison Key, Sis. Elena Harper, Rev. Jacqueline Farrow, Rev. Revita Dechalus, Min. Shirl Pernell, Lloyd Irving, Sylvester Rawlings, Rev. Dr. Raymond Bryant, Rev. Dr. Grainger Browning, and Rev. Dr. JoAnn Browning.

Inspired by my brother:
Determination...... to keep at it until you succeed in spite of all the problems and obstacles you will experience.

– Dr. Mateen Ajala Diop, Ed.D –

INTRODUCTION

Live life on purpose, in the midst of storms, trials, and tribulations. If at any time your peace and happiness was hindered because of emotional pain or physical abuse and you felt like giving up, this book will help you understand just who has all power in His hands.

I was abused throughout my childhood and teenage years by my stepfather and my mother. For many years, I blamed myself for everything I went through and started believing that I would never amount to anything. I heard these words so often from my family and neighbors. Yet, I'm still alive and living victoriously.

This is not a story of woe it's me or the blame game, but to share enough about my life to let you know that I understand what it means to feel hopeless, unwanted, and unloved. As I was growing up it didn't appear that God was anywhere near. How could he be? After all, I was being abused and nobody inquired on my behalf. But GOD!

I have gone through much in life from a young girl to adulthood. I didn't try to figure out why I was doing the things I did to people or to myself. I was just living and counted as sheep for the slaughter, but God had other plans. The enemy tried to take me out and put more on me than I could bear, but God said not so. I made it through the hell I endured. I made it through unwise choices and unhealthy relationships. Mavis will live and not die to declare the works of the Lord. God remained true to His Word that He has a plan for me to prosper and give me an expected end (Jeremiah 29:11).

God has inspired me to tell the truth in order to help those in similar situations come out of captivity. If you have never talked about your abuse or know someone that is being abused, I pray that reading this book will give you the courage to do so. The Lord has empowered me to teach spiritual development to people who have an ear to hear and are ready to let go of their past to move forward to a beautiful fulfilled life He has planned for them. God truly wants us to enjoy Him to the fullest.

As I share behavioral addictions caused by my own abuse, I will also reveal how God's unfailing love will show his amazing grace.

POEM

"I Was Lost and Felt All Alone"

Who will cry for the little girl lost and all alone?
Who will cry for the little girl abandoned without her own?
Who will cry for the little girl who cried herself to sleep?
Who will cry for the little girl who never had anything for keeps?
Who will cry for the little girl who walked the heated sun?
Who will cry for the little girl who's inside the woman?
Who will cry for the little girl who knew so much hurt and pain?
Who will cry for the little girl who died and died again?
Who will cry for the little girl a good girl she always tried to be?
Who will cry for the little girl who still cries inside of me?
Who will cry for the little girl who never had joy only rain?
Who will cry for the little girl who had nothing to gain?
Who will cry for the little girl who continues to wet the bed?
Who will cry for the little girl who was hit upside her head?
Who will cry for the little girl who still had to beg her brother?
Who will cry for the little girl who hated our mother?
Who will cry for the little girl who tried to run and hide?
Who will cry for the little girl with no one by her side?
Who will cry for the little girl who was whipped until she bled?
Who will cry for the little girl everyone wished was dead?
Who will cry for the little girl who said, "I can't stay, I got to get out?"
My brother cried for this little girl who knew what freedom was about.
I love my brother then, I love my brother now. I forgive you and I accept your apology. Nothing will ever separate us from the love of God or from each other.
Father God, thank you for never giving up on me. You Lord, cried for this little girl. I'm still here and yet I'm alive. Amen!

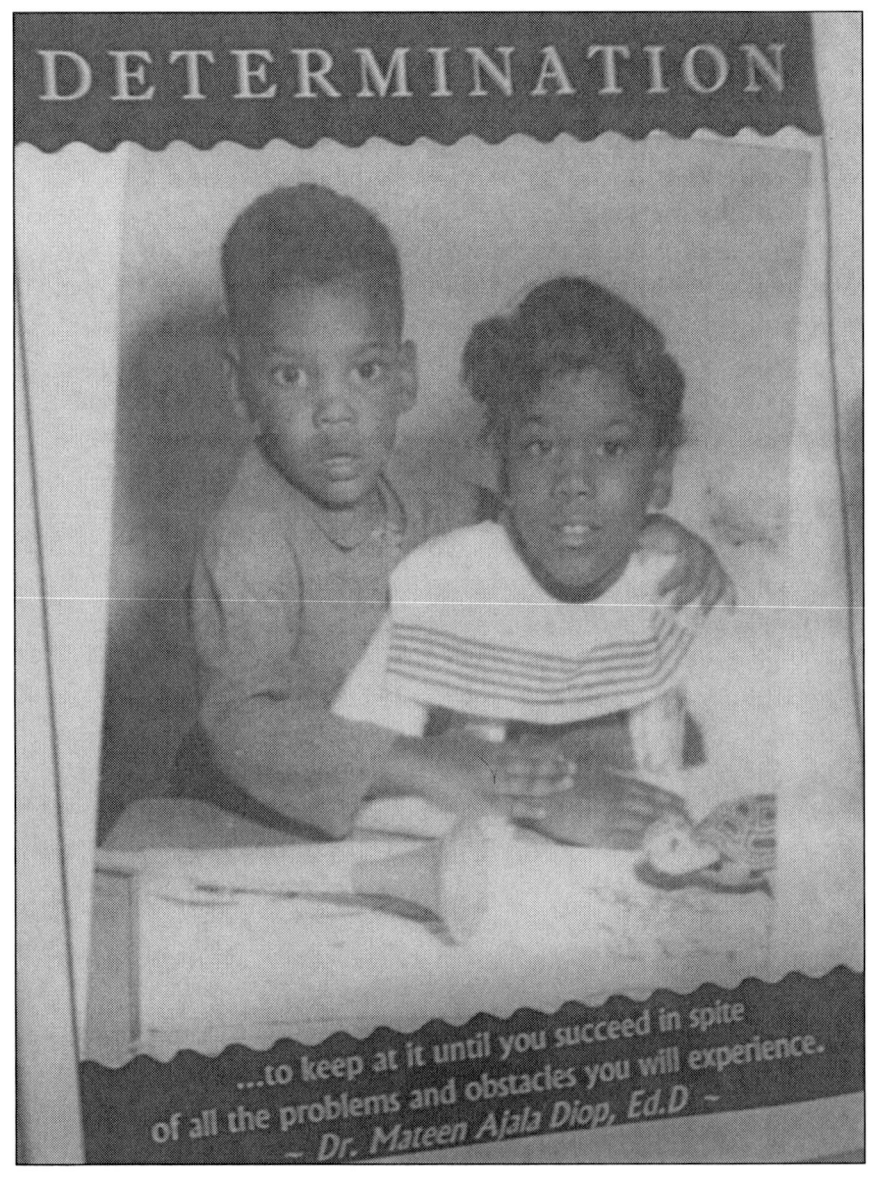

Mateen (Milton) and Mavis in our tender years.

FOREWORD

Congratulations mommy! I'm so proud of you. This is a great accomplishment. I hope you continue to write and publish books to help the body of Christ.

My prayer is that this book will inspire other people to write their stories.

Thank you for establishing a great legacy for your children by showing strength and love through very difficult times in your life.

I love you mommy and appreciate all you do to take care of me. If God be for us, who can be against us?

I dedicate these scriptures to you:

Galatians 6:9 Let us not become weary in doing good, for at the proper time we will reap a harvest if we do not give up.

Romans 6:23 "Our life is a gift from God, what we do with it is our gift to God."

Matthew 6:21 For where your treasure is, there your heart will be also.

Your daughter,

Adwoa Mylan Javeen Morisseau

"Broken, But Not Destroyed" is a moving reminder of the intricate web of human connection that somehow sustains us.

Pastor Mavis Morisseau fought to hold on through many rough and difficult times. She accomplished a will of God that has greatly enhanced the life she now lives. Pastor Mavis is the proud mother of eight beautiful children and four grandchildren. She is also a mentor who nurtures, guides, and challenges everyone to purpose to be better than yesterday in Christ Jesus.

As her older sister, I am so proud of her and admire her deeply. She has miraculously obtained a breakthrough which wasn't easy to do. Pastor Mavis has pulled through with excellence and guidance from the Word of God.

Mrs. Jocelyn Porter
Concierge
Washington, D.C.

When I was asked to write the foreword to Broken but not Destroyed for my dear friend, Mavis, I was extremely honored and proud that she would consider me for such a defining purpose in her intimate writings. I was also amazed at the unspeakable acts she had endured yet not letting them define the woman of God she is today.

I met Mavis over twenty-two years ago in Macon, Georgia. She and her family were stationed at Robins Air Force Base for a period of time. Mavis became a member of the community choir I sang with at the time, introducing herself and her five beautiful children to us at rehearsal. Since she was new in town and her husband was deployed at the time my godmother invited her and the kids over for our Friday night fish fry. I knew almost immediately that there was something special about this young lady because my godmother was catering to her like she was royalty. Little did I know at the time that she was to become one of God's anointed vessels.

She had the most beautiful children I had ever seen and because of my love for children and her needing a babysitter, our friendship developed quickly. Our time back then was spent singing, being in church and enjoying the many friends that came around. It was as if Mavis were a magnetic force that drew people to her. Wherever she went she commanded attention with her personality and smile.

Foreword

A smile that hid so many hurts, and pain that we never imagined the past in which she lived; a life that will be revealed in this book to share her story of abuse and forgiveness through God's love.

Life experiences and relocations caused Mavis and I to lose contact for about twenty years. When we reconnected God had elevated her to the role of a Pastor. When I saw her after all those years I knew God's hand was really at work in her life. This new Mavis still loved people but also had real joy in her heart. Not the mere happiness that comes and goes with each passing day but real joy and peace that only God could give. She no longer snapped at others or forced her strict motherhood on her nine year old daughter as she had with her now adult children. She cried out to the Lord with her whole heart and purposed Him in her life on a daily basis.

I had known a miniscule part of her childhood abuse but it was nothing compared to what she shared with me and what I read in her brother's book. In hearing and reading her story I was compelled to revisit some pains from my own past and find the peace of forgiveness that Pastor Mavis has now found. Through her authentic words in this book and its practical approaches in seeking God's guidance, you too can find the ability to forgive your abuser and have life abundantly, full of joy. Pastor Mavis' words of dealing with anger, fear, bitterness, instability and being ashamed are all emotions that every abuse victim has experienced. In her book she will help you move from the role of a victim to becoming victorious over the pain that has held you captive. I promise you this book has the capacity to change your life if you are willing to go through all of your emotions, face them head-on and allow God's healing power to restore you. Be Blessed!!!

Mrs. Michaelle Banks
Teacher & Friend
Macon, GA

PREFACE

Pastor Mavis Morisseau is family to me. She has been a part of my life for more than forty years. You see, that is how long I have been friends with her younger brother Mateen. We all grew up together in the same neighborhood and we ran the same streets. As we look back on those days, each of us counts our blessings for the lives we live today. Of course back then she was simply Mavis and she was a pistol. All I can say is that she is the last person that I thought one day would have title of pastor. But with all that is going on in the world today I am certainly pleased that Pastor Morisseau is on the scene. And as the story of her life has unfolded no one is better suited to minister to our people on how to survive the trials and tribulations of life than Mavis.

Mavis has been through her share of pain. I am so proud of her and I have told her so often when we have had occasions to visit recently. She is my shero. When we were growing up I can remember that she always seemed to be angry and ready to fight at the drop of a hat. And everyone knew it. They also knew that if you messed with her brother Mateen (and by association me) then you messed with her. And that was not something most wanted to deal with. Moreover, she always seemed to be very loud and quick tempered. I am laughing as I write this because I as I write this I am realizing how she was only expressing herself back then and dealing with things the best way she knew how. It all makes sense now. I am overjoyed because as she has found peace and learned to forgive she has allowed Pastor Mavis to emerge. Pastor Mavis is a kinder, gentler, and sweeter version of the Mavis I knew growing up. I realize now that this is the real Mavis.

The Mavis I never knew growing up because I only knew the shell, the defense mechanism that was in place as a survival tactic. It has been a long road for her and it has taken years for Mavis to become the woman and leader she is today and her life's journey is a testament to the strength and the will of the human spirit. And when you mesh that will with a strong faith and dedication to God, well then anything is possible. More recently, her brother and I have seen more of her as we have traveled to our nation's capital recently on several occasions and each time we made it a point to visit with her. A few years back Mateen published his first book and of course Mavis was there to support him. She delivered an awe-inspiring dance performance as a tribute to him in honor of his accomplishments. As I stated at the outset, Mavis has been through much. Her transformation from the angry teenager I knew on the streets of San Antonio, Texas to the woman she is today is nothing short of miraculous. I am thrilled to play this small role in bringing her triumphant story to the world.

Kai Ajala Dupé
September 2014
Houston, Texas

1

Our Inner Life with God

No longer chained and shackled to my past, the skeletons in my closet are released and curses cease. I am free, and destined to walk in liberty.
Rev. Stephanie Harley

A significant number of children in American society are exposed to traumatic life events. A traumatic event is one that threatens injury, death, or the physical integrity of self or others and also causes horror, terror, or helplessness at the time it occurs. Immediately after the event, shock and denial are typical. Longer term reactions include unpredictable emotions, flashbacks, strained relationships and even physical symptoms. While these feelings are normal, some people have difficulty moving on with their lives. The victims of trauma do not understand what is wrong with them, or how to stop destructive behavior patterns. That was me before I gained victory over trauma in my life.

Through seeking God and reading His word, the Lord's main concern is our inner life because that is where we enjoy His presence. Our inner life is our heart, mind, and soul. All we are and destined to be is because of God reigning on the inside of us. Jesus said, "Behold, the kingdom of God is within you" (Luke 17:21). He has given you everything you need to triumph and succeed in life.

God taught me how to triumph over my tragedy. I began to succeed by placing my issues in His hand and allowing Him to lead. I could not do it by myself, but with God even the smallest victories were grand. I am reminded of 2 Corinthians 2:14: "But thanks be to God, who always leads us as captives in Christ's triumphal procession and uses us to spread the aroma of the knowledge of him everywhere." My life has progressed for the better because I made a conscious decision to live God's way. Daily I died to self and grew spiritually as I surrendered all of me to Him. By all of me I'm referring to any issue, hurt, pain, offense, sin, unforgiveness, bitterness, and anything this is not pleasing to God in my life. I let go of the self-destruction and replaced it with life.

I was transformed to a champion in life by practicing Godly habits and discipline. Just like some of our old habits became second nature to us because we have done them over and over (like smoking, drinking, or cursing), I began practicing disciplines of *Bible study, prayer, meditation, worship, and fasting*. I chose to live and not die to declare the works of the Lord (Psalm 118:17).

God is the Champion at bringing people from a place of destruction to a place of total victory. As our lives transform every day, it is a reminder of how powerful and great God's goodness and mercy is towards us. I am a living testimony of someone who should have been dead a long time ago, but God! I am one of the trophies in His kingdom. I survived and I win in Christ. I share my testimony for those who are still in the process of becoming a winner and an overcomer for God.

In my quest to survive, I had to understand that Jesus is my all and all. He had to be my everything. Apart from Him we are nothing and susceptible to anything the enemy throws our way. God wants you to make him your everything to where you can't eat, sleep, or breathe without Him. He desires to reign and rule in your inner life-our mind, will, emotions, thoughts, and desires. God wants our will to line up with His will. If God has captured these areas of your life, then you are on your way to serving Him in a way that is acceptable and pleasing.

As believers, we have God in us. If God's kingdom rules within us then we will enjoy peace, righteousness, and joy in the Holy Spirit.

We won't be anxious for anything because God will make provision. The Word of God says in Matthew 6:33, "But seek ye first the kingdom of God, and his righteousness; and all these things shall be added unto you." Seek the Kingdom of God first which is within us, and God will provide for other concerns. An important emphasis here is the word *within*. Our inner man has to be whole and healed before we can experience this joy and peace in an outward life. There has to be a change on the inside for the outer man to be renewed. If this transformation and renewal in the heart and mind takes place we will not only survive, but you will truly enjoy your lives.

Our inner life with God is so important because our heart, mind, and will resides there. When one has been abused, all of the three need healing and redirecting through the Word of God. Getting to the heart of the issue is a process. Therefore, we must work patience and perseverance while change is occurring. Patience because in traumatic and life changing experiences, it takes time to release and let go of hurt. It takes time to truly forgive and it takes time to come from a place of brokenness. Exercise perseverance because you have to endure your process to come out healthy and whole. Though some of us seem to have suffered unbearable pain, Jesus came to set us free. In Luke 4:18 the scripture says, "He has sent me to proclaim freedom for the prisoners and recovery of sight for the blind, to set the oppressed free, to proclaim the year of the Lord's favor." Jesus came to heal the broken hearted, those broken into pieces inwardly.

No matter how traumatic the abuse, God has been there all along. He just wants you to take hold of Him and call on Him in the name of Jesus. Look at Job, he had a devastating season in his life. Satan did everything he could think to do to destroy Job. Job had friends around that spoke against his beliefs. He began to look at the circumstances of life and forget the power of God. God had to regain Job's attention. When Job acknowledged God and his own sin, then he was back on track. As he remained steadfast in his faithfulness to God he prevailed. Job's outcome was victory. The Lord turned the captivity of Job when he prayed for his friends (Job 42:10). Victory comes when you release what you have been harboring for years. God will do the same for you when you release your offender.

My prayer is that God will strengthen your inner man through the power of the Holy Spirit and that he will dwell boldly and confidently in your heart, mind, and spirit. The Lord will keep you in perfect peace because he will never leave you or forsake you (He will not give up on you or leave you without support). Your mouth shall speak, "the Lord is my helper, I will not be afraid." What can man do to me (Hebrews 13:5-6)?

2

Residue of Abuse

"When purpose is not known, abuse is inevitable"
Dr. Myles Munroe

Some common forms of abuse are: physical, verbal, mental, emotional, and sexual. At some point in most people's lives they have experienced one or the other. Abuse means to deceive, wrong or improper use, maltreat, excessive use, and language that condemns and defile. In traumatic experiences one may have had all of the forms of abuse inflicted on them. This is severe abuse.

Any form of ongoing abuse produces a root of rejection in the individual who has been mistreated and a sense of unworthiness. This together can cause major problems in an individual's relationship and interpersonal relationships. This is the cause of many people not getting along with one another. There are hurt and abused people who don't want to be hurt again. Although the abuse has stopped, the residue of their trauma lingers on and affects their ability to relate to others. I'm a testament to that. Most people that I have developed relationships with, I hurt. What I took in from years of abuse is what I gave out. Even if they were my friends.

The enemy works daily to prey on people dealing with rejection and unworthiness because he wants to keep you in that state. If he can keep you in that place, then you can't develop Godly friendships, relationships, or families. The devil comes to steal, kill, and destroy (John 10:10). If you have been abused, then most likely you will abuse someone else. If you have been abandoned, then you will abandon someone. The hurt, hurts other people and most times you don't see the damage caused until it's done.

Abuse, whether from abandonment, broken relationships, divorce, false accusations, exclusion from groups, molestation, dislike by teachers and authority figures, or other hurtful actions can and do cause emotional scars that prevent people in their efforts to maintain healthy relationships.

God created us for love and acceptance. Love, because He is love. We love because he first loved us and whoever claims to love God, but yet hate his brother or sister is a liar (1John4:16, 19-20). As I looked at myself in my abusive state, my actions toward people or God didn't line up with what my mouth was saying.

I always praised the Lord and told him how much I loved Him. Love and kind words were coming out of my mouth yet abusive behavior was still present. I needed to be healed of the pain of abuse and I had to want to get well. We have to choose to accept God (every part of Him) and let go of dwelling in darkness, then we can truly love and truly be accepted because of the love that resides on the inside of us. The God kind of love and acceptance is stated in Matthew 22:37-40 *37 Jesus replied: "Love the Lord your God with all your heart and with all your soul and with all your mind. 38 This is the first and greatest commandment. 39 And the second is like it: 'Love your neighbor as yourself." 40 All the Law and the Prophets hang on these two commandments."* You have to be determined to get to a place in your life where you can give love and know how to receive love.

Mistreated and Abused?

Being mistreated and abused can deeply affect your emotional state. Are you an emotional prisoner? Have you been bound and locked up inside for years? Let us look at the woman with the issue of blood. Mark 5:25- 29 *KJV* says, *"And a certain woman which had an issue of blood for twelve years. 26 and had suffered many things from many physicians. She had spent all that she had and was no better, but rather grew worse. 27 When she had heard of Jesus, came in the press behind, and touched his garment. 28 For she said, if I may touch but his clothes, I shall be whole." 29 And straightway the fountain of her blood was dried up; and she felt in her body that she was healed of that plague.* Other versions of the Bible state her condition as hemorrhage, constant bleeding, chronic bleeding, and discharge of blood. Women with blood issues during these times were considered unclean because of the disease. You were considered unclean during the menstrual cycle. How about bleeding all the time? Can you imagine the stigma that followed her because of the disease? Can you imagine the name calling, the rejection, abandonment, or even exclusion from society? She tried multiple avenues to be healed according to the world's means by getting treated by physicians and that didn't work. She spent all she had. She was searching for relief and wanted to be free from not only sickness and disease, but also of hurt and pain. I'm sure she was tired of being sick and lived off of her last bit of hope. When her opportunity came, the woman seized it. She pressed her way through the crowd to touch Jesus. The woman reached out to Jesus in faith and was healed immediately. Doctors couldn't heal her, but her faith in God through Jesus did. What's amazing about her deliverance is that when her resources ran out, God's resource kicked in.

The door was opened for healing because the woman said something. She said, "If I may only touch his clothes, I shall be made well." She said and she acted, then God responded. The woman yearned for healing in her heart all she needed to do was add words of faith and it was as good as done. You see faith doesn't include doubt. She knew that she would be healed. The heart, her words, and action lined up with God's Word. If you ask and believe, you will receive (Mark 11:22-24). Secondly, she told Jesus the truth when he asked, "Who touched me?" It is the will of Christ that his people should be comforted, and He has power to command comfort to troubled spirits. The more simply we depend on Him, and expect great things from him, the more we shall find in ourselves that he has become our salvation. Those who, by faith, are healed of their spiritual diseases, have reason to go in peace. You too can be healed and live life in peace and holiness.

Do you want to get well? Do you want it bad enough to do what is required of you? You have the right to get out of the prison that you're in. Many people that are in prison function, but are not free. They have become accustomed to the bondage and it actually feels quite normal. They have adapted to living in their condition. However, Jesus came to open the doors and set the captives free, to bind up wounds and hurts, and heal broken hearts. If you want to be free and if you want to be well, Jesus wants to heal you. He is ready, are you?

Laying Down the Burden

Laying down the emotional bondage from abuse is not easy. It's a process that you have to be willing to work through. For most people, it's very uncomfortable to bring up their past and speak about what really happened to them. Many have never talked about their abusive situation because they begin to see it as if it happened yesterday. You see the abuse and you see the person who did it. To remember and discuss these events hurts you all over again so you'd rather not speak about it. It provokes feelings and emotions that you don't want to face.

Maybe you tried to speak about your experience on a previous occasion and it was too hurtful. Therefore, you backed down and told the Lord you weren't ready yet. At some point, you have to be ready to deal with what others have done to you so that you can overcome the trauma and be well. God can't use you at your full potential in a broken and damaged state. It's your responsibility to be well because God said, you already win. He has the final say. Do you get it? You win
and it's up to you to know that for yourself. If life was going to be over for you, you wouldn't be reading this book now.

But you are here, still living and breathing, waking up to His sunrise, going to work in the morning, going to church on Sunday, Bible study during the week, raising children, going to college, and so on. You hear His trumpet sound every morning and you wake up, that's God. Face this so called giant in your life and move on. Own up to who you are and your emotional baggage. Stop dumping it on others because you are not well. Choose not to spend one more day bound to unforgiveness, repressed anger, self-pity, a chip-on-the shoulder, or that someone-owes- me "big time" attitude.

The Poet Langston Hughes said in his poem, A Dream Deferred;

What happens to a dream deferred?
Does it dry up like a raisin in the sun?
Or fester like a sore—
And then run?
Does it stink like rotten meat?
Or crust and sugar over—
like a syrupy sweet?
Maybe it just sags like a heavy load.
Or does it explode?

I read the meaning of the verses in this well-known poem. However, this time when reading it, the Holy Spirit told me that this is what an abused person goes through. Listen, is your purposed life on hold, a vision deferred? You know it's there, but can't access it? Is your reservoir of joy at its lowest level? It's always dry and temporary. Does your anger fester, infect and leave a bad taste to those around you? Do you know how to hold on to good friends? Or do you create a false image that all is well almost as this was meant to be? You act like everything is peaches and cream and put on a front every day. Maybe you will just let all this pain, anger, and emotional burden wear you down until you explode.

This is what happens if you don't let go of the baggage. A cleansing and gutting out of all these venomous behaviors have to cease in order for you to be well. Set your mind on the affections of God because you may never get that apology you've been waiting for, that request for forgiveness, or that love you longed for from a mother, father, uncle, or brother. It may be a long time coming, but in the meantime, God says, "Here I am. What about me?" Give your whole self to God and allow Him to mesmerize you with His Love. Nobody can love you like God! When you know that, then you are on your way.

I urge you to be confident and know that God is rooting and cheering for you. Every step you take to overcome He is ecstatic. You might ask me, "How do you know?" First, the scripture in Philippians 1:6 says, "being confident of this very thing, that He who has begun a good work in you will complete it until the day of Jesus Christ." Second, Romans 8:28 states, "And we know that all things work together for good to those who love God, to those who are the called according to His purpose." And third, for the Holy Spirit, Zephaniah 3:17 The Lord your God in your midst, The Mighty One, will save; He will rejoice over you with gladness, He will quiet you with His love, He will rejoice over you with singing."

If you made the choice to face your past and are determined to take the necessary steps to get well, let's move forward.

3

A Recurring Cycle

"The Buck Stops Here"

"I believe that we are solely responsible for our choices, and we have to accept the consequences of every deed, word, and thought throughout our lifetime." Elisabeth Kubler-Ross

Trauma experienced in one generation of a family can affect generations to come. This occurs when there has been physical, sexual and emotional abuse of children, neglect of children and domestic violence.

Adults who were physically abused as children can develop into parents who physically abuse their own children. Childhood physical abuse is most often perpetrated under the disguise of providing discipline for the children who are abused. Consequently, children who experience physical abuse can come to believe that abusive tactics are appropriate ways to teach and discipline children. Additionally, adults who were physically abused as children may form adult relationships in which there is domestic violence. This cycle of abuse is spiritual wickedness. Abuse being passed down from generation to generation is a generational curse. For example, Great grandma was abused, grandma was abused, mother was abused by grandma, and now you and your sibling are victims of abuse. When a victim of abuse is asked, "why did you inflict abuse on someone?" many will say, "that's what I knew to do and that's what was done to me." It doesn't make the abuse right by any means, however, the abuser has been taught to do it and live with it and believe that everything is going to be all right.

In reality nothing is going to be alright because inside of an abused person is a ticking bomb waiting to explode.

Just to show you how a generation curse operates in a family, let's look at David in 2 Samuel Chapter 11. Here I'm paraphrasing what happens. It was a time of battle and Israel had defeated the people of Ammon and continued to Rabbah, but David decides to stay in Jerusalem. David sees Bathsheba bathing and finds her attractive. So, he orders his men to go get her even though she is married. When she arrived, David slept with Bathsheba.

Sometime later she informed David that conception had taken place and that she is with child. Therefore, David first plotted to cover his sin by telling Uriah to come in from war and go home hoping that he would sleep with Bathsheba. When David's plans were not successful David sent word to Joab by letter to set Uriah up to die in battle. Set Uriah on the front line in the worst place and leave him there to die. David had Uriah killed. When David did this, he set in motion curses and catastrophes to happen in his family.

Now here's the generational curse in David's family: 2 Samuel 12:10-11

10 Now therefore the sword shall never depart from thine house; because thou hast despised me, and hast taken the wife of Uriah the Hittite to be thy wife. 11 Thus saith the Lord, Behold, I will raise up evil against thee out of thine own house, and I will take thy wives before thine eyes, and give them unto thy neighbour, and he shall lie with thy wives in the sight of this sun. A curse of evil, disrespect, tragedy, misfortune, affliction, and a constant threat of murder will take place throughout David's family because of his sin. These events take place during David's life:

1. David's wives given to someone close to him in broad daylight.
2. David's son died even though he confessed and repented.
3. Tamar gets raped by her brother Ammon.
4. Absalom has his brother (Ammon) killed.

Get the point? You can see the cycle of abuse, disrespect, murder, and death happening in the family. Now look at your situation and your family history. Does abuse of any kind run in your family? Did your abuser come from a dysfunctional background? If you can say "yes" to these questions, then it's time to declare that the buck stops here and now!

If you realize that you have been living under generational curses, you have a choice to make. You can choose to let go of the past and live or keep living in a destructive cycle and die. I know these are strong words, but it's the truth and it's the Word. Deuteronomy 30:15-19 *says, 15 See, I have set before thee this day life and good, and death and evil; 16 In that I command thee this day to love the Lord thy God, to walk in his ways, and to keep his commandments and his statutes and his judgments, that thou mayest live and multiply: and the Lord thy God shall bless thee in the land whither thou goest to possess it. 17 But if thine heart turn away, so that thou wilt not hear, but shalt be drawn away, and worship other gods, and serve them; 18 I denounce unto you this day, that ye shall surely perish, and that ye shall not prolong your days upon the land, whither thou passest over Jordan to go to possess it. 19 I call heaven and earth to record this day against you, <u>that I have set before you life and death, blessing and cursing</u>: <u>therefore choose life, that both thou and thy seed may live.</u>*

God sets before you good, death, and evil. Sin is evil and evil leads to death. Abusive behavior leads to death (John 6:*23For the wages of sin is death*). Stop this destructive cycle for you and your family. Choose to live today because someone's life depends on you.

Don't Ignore the Warning Signs

Many times when we are not well our bodies will give us a warning message that something is not right. A warning can come in the sign of a headache, back ache, muscle tension, joint pain, nose bleeds, migraines, loss of hair, stomach issues, heart problems, and much more. Have you ever thought about sin being connected to sickness? They both work hand in hand. We just read the scripture in John that said sin lead to death. When your body gives you a warning, check out how you are living. It's your wake up call to change something in your life. The change that needs to take place is both physical and spiritual.

One may take prescribed medicine to alleviate their pain. Sometimes it will work. But hurt and illness that is deep-rooted within needs spiritual healing as well. You can be healed if you don't ignore the warning signs.

I will share a little about the warning I encountered. God gave me a grand awakening one evening. In 2009, I had a fairly good day so it seemed. I had been experiencing some headaches, but ignored them. Also, I told no one about them. I spent that evening relaxing in the bathtub while talking to a friend. When I decided to stand and get out of the tub, halfway up I got dizzy and sat back down. Within seconds, blood began to drip from my nose. My friend and I began to hold my head back and pinch my nose to try and clot the blood to stop it. That didn't work this time as it had in the past and blood came out of my mouth as well. I had a prior nose bleed and was able to stop it so I felt initially there was nothing to be alarmed about. This time the blood kept coming and the ambulance was called. By the time the Emergency Response Team arrived, the flow of blood had minimized, but my blood pressure was high. I was driven to the hospital that night and examined. The doctor could not find anything and basically administered some type of superficial treatment (since they really didn't see anything) by burning tissue in my nose to help clot any blood. I was released and went home that night. I woke up the next day with my nose bleeding all over again. Every time I sat up on the bed or tried to get up from a lying position blood flowed. My friend and I were using rolls of tissue to wipe the blood and dispose of it in plastic bags. It was too much blood and we decided to drive to a different hospital this time. My nose was examined by the ER doctors and they came to no conclusion, only to give me a prescription to start blood pressure medication.

My friend told doctors that I really needed to stay because something was wrong and if we go home that it would start again. However, we were told by the staff to go home and that I would be fine. Well, I went back to that same hospital several more times because the bleeding didn't stop and they put a ballooned device in my nose to clot the blood and I went home. That didn't work. Needless to say, I was tired and my friends were tired of seeing me go through this.

I had been losing blood for a week now and doctors wouldn't admit me for treatment. My last episode that week blood poured out of my nose and mouth. I was rushed once again to the hospital. This time the hospital admitted me but still had no clue as to what was causing the bleeding. All the time that my nose was bleeding I was also swallowing blood. This was a horrific ordeal.

During my treatment while at the hospital, the ballooned device was in my nose and a tube suctioning the blood from my mouth. The cup on the side of the bed filled with deep dark red blood. Doctors had started me on blood pressure medication that would possibly stabilize everything that was going on. I was having the worst migraine and felt my brain was about to explode. I was getting weary, tired, and ready to give up. My family and friends, those important in my life during this time, gathered in my room and prayed for me. Later, I told my best friend who had been there with me, "if the pain doesn't stop, I'm going to pull this tube out of my nose and my arms and I'm done."

The doctors came back in my room later that evening for observations. They made a decision to try one last option to stop the bleeding and if that didn't work then I would go into surgery. The doctor came in my room with his little black bag and medical staff. I had only seen those types of bags on television. It looked like he was making a house call like doctors did years ago. My friend was asked to leave my side although I wanted her to stay. I can't recall what the doctor did, but the procedure wasn't long at all and afterward I felt so much better. I was so relieve of the migraine and pain. Praise God! I went hours without having any dripping of blood. My pressure was getting stabilized. Yes! We can rest well and get some sleep.

All was well and I made it through the night. I made it half way through the next day and....more blood. I sunk back into a depression and figured it was my time to leave this world. I was ready to say goodbye. But, God said, "No, That was just a warning for you to get your life together and I'm giving you another chance because I love you and your work is not done." I did not bleed anymore and a few days later I was released to go home.

God told me what all of this meant. I had so much sin in my life from abuse and bad blood that had been passed onto me through generational curses, that I needed cleansing and purging. Every ounce of bad blood had to leave my body so that God could replace it with his blood, pure and Holy.

I lost so much blood that I should have needed a transfusion. But the Lord was replenishing me with brand new blood from Him. I thank the Lord every day that He allowed me to go through that. I also thank the Lord for choosing to bring me out, because He didn't have too. Jehovah Rapha gave me an opportunity to start over. I left the hospital and the process to change my heart, mind, and direction began. I was broken, but not destroyed. Thank you Jesus!

God gives you warnings also. If a red flag is waving in front of your face just surrender. It comes to a point in your life where you are accountable for your actions. You can no longer blame mama, daddy, uncle, or whomever for what you choose to do. Don't allow evil acts done to you keep you in bondage for years. You have to want to do the right thing and live Holy (Leviticus 11:44-45 *For I am Yahweh your God, so you must consecrate yourselves and be holy because I am holy). You must not defile yourselves by any swarming creature that crawls on the ground. 45 For I am Yahweh, who brought you up from the land of Egypt to be your God, so you must be holy because I am holy*). Make a decision that anything that is not like God in your life you have to let it go. If your life doesn't please God, then change. Change and destroy the curse in your family or the curse will destroy you. Surrender your all to God.

- Romans 12:2–And be not conformed to this world: but be ye transformed by the renewing of your mind, that ye may prove what [is] that good, and acceptable, and perfect, will of God.
- James 4:7–Submit yourselves therefore to God. Resist the devil, and he will flee from you.

4

Rotten Roots

You may have heard of the term "rotten to the core". It is synonymous to other words like: canker (evil), debauched, godless, heinous, scandalous, villainous, and wicked. The core of fruit is the central part of it containing the seeds. So if the seed which produces the fruit is rotten, then the fruit will be rotten. Abusive addictive behaviors don't just show up in someone's life out of nowhere. There was a process to get that seed planted. Once planted, the seed of abuse was massaged, nurtured, and watered over and over again. It has a source, which has a root; a rotten root and rotten soil. Rotten fruit leads to abusive addictive behavior in which hurt is not only inflicted on friends and family, but the victim himself. A victim of abuse has a tendency to put themselves in danger by living unhealthy lives. Oftentimes they set themselves up to receive more abuse through habits such as: deceitfulness, cheating, stealing, prostitution, adultery, and suicide. To deal with behavioral addictions caused by abuse, we have to take a look at the root of one's issues.

In my own life I had a lot of bad fruit sprouting on my branches. If I could have corrected my addictive behavior myself, I would have. Although I had tried, I was only pulling at the weeds and never pulling up the roots. If the roots are not pulled up then the roots just create a new crop of problems.

Thoughts that are planted in the mind:

- Is something wrong with me?
- If I can't get a good feeling from the inside of me, I will get it from somewhere else on the outside.
- The real me isn't acceptable
- My addictions make me feel good even if the feeling is only temporary

A diagram of outward behavioral addictions

- Controlling, Stealing
- Manipulation, Rebellion
- Judgemental, Covetousness
- Pretend Me
- Anger, Hostility, Deception
- Sex, Money, Power
- Improper imaging from parents/ Rejection

The root of behavioral addictions is; abuse, coupled with shame, guilt, and rejection. They are satan's best tools to tear a person to pieces spiritually. Shame and guilt robs you of your faith, joy, peace, confidence, and pure conscience. You find it hard to talk about your struggles to anyone, especially sexual sins. Sexual sins have a strong hold on people. It's not just the fleshly nature of the sin, but rather the working of unclean spirits. Shame and guilt causes you to cover up and hide like Adam and Eve did in the Garden of Eden. In Genesis 3:10 Adam said, *"I heard thy voice in the garden, and I was afraid, because I was naked; and I hid myself."* Then God said in verse 11, *"Who told thee that thou wast naked?"* Before this Adam and Eve didn't know about nakedness. Thus, unclean spirits were speaking to them. Shame and guilt can cause dread and fear which ultimately makes someone want to distance themselves from God. So why do unclean spirits work so hard to keep a person 'locked up/bound' concerning their failure or struggle? He does not want them to open up and uncover the darkness in their soul in which guilt and shame have their strongest grip.

God's Word is clear that confessing our faults to one another can bring about and promote healing in one's life: James 5:16, *"Confess your faults one to another, and pray one for another, that ye may be healed. The effectual fervent prayer of a righteous man availeth much."*

Another bad root that causes addictive behavior is rejection. Rejection is a refusal to show someone the love and kindness that they need or expect. As a child, if you are not hugged, encouraged, told that you are loved and that you matter, you can feel a sense of rejection. Receiving bad treatment is rejection. It doesn't make you feel good about who you are.

The act of rejection can make the person experiencing it undergo a sudden drop in positive emotion. This is displayed as something ranging from a vague disappointment, sadness, and depression, to anxiety, and phobic behavior. When an act of physical violence is thrust upon a person, the first reaction is to protect oneself. The hands go up and cover the face or vital areas; the upper body leans away in order to retreat from the pain that is being inflected. It is almost as if there is a force pulling the body away from the impending danger. Psychologists have researched brain activity while studying emotional rejection and found that the brain registers the same pain as physical abuse. When we are hurt emotionally the same reaction occurs internally; our mental and emotional states are looking to move away from the hurtful person or situation, just as a person under attack. These are responses of defense and the subconscious mind does not differentiate between physical and emotional pain, as both can hurt us.

When we experience enough situations of hurt, we feel we have to protect our self from further hurt.

Addictions as a result of rejection can be: drugs and alcohol, food, sex, desire for acceptance, pornography, spending and shopping, loneliness, depression, and a life of deception. Look at Tamar's story in Genesis chapter 38. She was married to Judah's first son Er. When Er died because of sin, she was given to the second son, Onan. Onan didn't want any children by Tamar, he also sinned and died. Judah rejected the idea of the third son marrying Tamar because he thought the youngest would die also, so he sent Tamar home to her father rejected (Genesis 38:11). Rejection, shame, hurt, and desire for acceptance caused Tamar to deceive Judah and sleep with him.

What is the true root of your behavioral addictions? What is your beginning that you have kept hidden? Pull it up by the root and expose it. Exposure can bring about closure.

5

My World

The Beginning

"True forgiveness is when you can say, "Thank you for that experience." Oprah Winfrey

As a little girl, I grew up in San Antonio, Texas. I never knew that all of my struggles and pain really started in a town called Hemsted and Caldwell, Texas where my mother's family was born. She was born to Elsie and Willie Lee and throughout her years of growing up, mother was a loner. My mother came from a generation of street fighters (her mother and her mother's mother were fighters) so, naturally fighting passed on to her. Mother didn't start a fight, but she sure would finish it. Eventually, my mother left home at a young age after being mistreated on so many levels, saying, "I just can't take it anymore."

As I spoke with my mother to get an understanding of her childhood, it revealed much hurt and pain. Her father's punishment was a beating with a 2 by 4 piece of wood by his grandmother which caused him to become deaf in one ear. Seems no one had experienced real parental love. Consequently, mother never received love or nurture from her parents so she didn't have loving, nurturing traits with her children. How could she? She was only doing what she knew: anger, frustration, hatred, and verbal abuse.

As a teenager starting her menstrual cycle, my mother was not told how to handle development change in life so she went to a neighbor's house. The elderly woman instructed her to go to W.H. Leornard grocery store to get the necessities. There were lonely times for her and it was as if she was raising herself.

During this time in mother's life it was a dark world. Her mother and father never said I love you. They made sure she had lunch money and knew when to be home. When the relationship didn't work out between her mother and father, she couldn't succumb to the orders of her stepfather or stepmother so she left home, got a room, a job, and supported herself.

At the age of fourteen, mother married C.L. Ladson, a military man. As time went on year after year, there were more marriages and more children. I, Mavis, needed to know why she had children if she was unhappy and bitter in life. My mother explained the vicissitudes of her life from childhood to adulthood.

I cried many tears listening to the hate, malice, bitterness, jealousy, unforgiveness, and pride that dwelled inside of her because that stench of sin spilled over to all of her children.

Understanding that phase of my mother's life definitely helped me reflect over the hurt received in my own life. It affected how I raised my own children and chose to live my life.

My Childhood

During my childhood, living in the house was two younger brothers, my mother and stepfather. I was doing great in elementary school and was getting all S's (for satisfactory). I was doing well and loved by many at school, I thought. My mother was very popular in the community and known for her bad attitude. She could curse you out at the drop of a dime. If something went wrong, everyone knew about it.

My family was musically inclined so I used to dance and sing with the older siblings. We entertained our family members who came to the house every weekend to smoke, drink, and gamble. If we were sleep, mom would call us to get up to entertain our relatives or friends. I was in my night gown and it didn't matter to her. I would sit on men laps and think it was normal. I didn't know how inappropriate that really was when I was young.

My stepfather controlled my mother and everyone in the house. His anger was severe and he used to beat mother often until her face was swollen and disfigured. He also broke her arm, threw ash trays at her, and screamed and beat her. After everything was said and done, they laid in the bed as if nothing ever happened. This went on for years.

In 1975, my stepfather asked me, "Do you want five dollars?" I said, "Yes". He gave me five dollars to go buy whatever I wanted from the store. The next day on a Monday night (I can remember this like it was yesterday) he came to me and said, "I want to show you something and don't tell anyone or you know what will happen!" The first encounter with him was touching his private parts and sitting on his lap to feel his private part rub against me. This went on for a while until he summoned me to come in on a Wednesday (from outside playing with my friends) to lie down. My stepfather forced obscene acts upon me in their bedroom. For years this physical abuse continued. Due to the abuse that was happening at home, my grades began to decline along with my behavior. No one ever asked what is going on with Mavis, as I was fighting every day, lying, stealing, and getting in all kinds of trouble. Why didn't anyone care? Why me? I felt I was left behind to wither and die.

There were days that I would go across the street to the smokehouse to get food so that I wouldn't have to be home. I had a friend who was an older gentleman who never touched me inappropriately. He gave me and my brothers food and money. He gave often so I never had to ask my stepfather or mother for money or anything. I had every color of converse tennis shoes that was out and my brothers and I also went to the movies often to see Bruce Lee movies. Sometimes I would go to the gas station to get sodas and chips just to be around my neighbors, anywhere, but not home.

I left home one early afternoon to hang out with friends in another neighborhood. I didn't make it back home in time before the street lights turned on. The street lights are on and I'm running down the street. I hear my mother calling, "Mavis Evette!" I knew I was in trouble. I must say, my mother did have a method to what kind of beatings I was going to get. She would either use a belt, extension cord, or a water hose most of the time. I got them all very often. I got in trouble for fighting in school every day if it was said that I started the fight. I couldn't win for losing.

I got pregnant at a very early age by my stepfather. I remember my sister hoping that I had a tumor inside. My mother and cousin took me to have an abortion. However, the abuse continued. My life was so messed up I didn't know whether I was coming or going. I smoked marijuana, drank, and took pills as often as it was given to me to take away the pain. I cried out for help so many times and no one ever listened. Back in those days it was about keeping your man happy, not your children.

Skeletons in My Closet

*"There is no greater agony than bearing
An untold story inside of you."*
Maya Angelou

We lived in a three bedroom shotgun house. This was the label for most of the homes in our neighborhood because if you shot a gun from your front door the bullet would travel all the way to the back without touching anything else. I was known in the neighborhood as the one in the family who would fight at the drop of a dime. I didn't need much swaying, just one wrong word and I lost my mind. You were hit in the face. I was also known to be "fast" meaning promiscuous along with foul-mouthed, and the girl with discipline problems.

As I grew older I began wetting the bed nightly. I would beg my brother Milton to allow me to sleep in bed with him. It seemed strange to him for me to ask because I had my own room and bed. Every night I continued to beg to sleep with him and he always told me no. He didn't want me wetting his bed. So, I cried as I fearfully went to my own room. Fear was a constant companion: I feared my stepfather, his anger, and my mother finding out what was happening. I needed to be rescued, but by whom? Who could I tell without making things worse?

I got into fights daily at school. One incident in particular is when I was walking home from school and three neighborhood girls who were sisters confronted me. I began swinging my fist and struck one of the girls. One of them grabbed me so I took hold the other sister's hair and held one down with my foot while still swinging at the third sister. An event of this magnitude was daily.

My behavior was sporadic, erratic, and more. One day I could be the nicest person in the world and the next day someone could get a beating they would never forget. No one really knew what triggered the behavior, but one day my brother, Milton, remembered seeing my stepfather walk past his room and into my room. He didn't think much of it at the time, he just knew that I was crying and thought I had received a spanking for erratic behavior. Sometime I would take my anger out on my brothers also. So, to get a spanking at strange hours of the night was not uncommon.

During this time, our mother was a bowler. She spent many nights away from home participating in tournaments, so we were left with our stepfather. My stepfather visited my room at odd hours many nights for a long time. I eventually told Milton that our stepfather was hurting me. At first, he was shocked. I confided in Milton all of the instances of abuse. I reminded him of the time I had to leave school and go to the doctor. I told him I went to get an abortion. I was barely twelve or thirteen at this time. I told Milton how our stepfather would have prophylactics on his clothes dresser and day-by-day the number of them would shrink. My stepfather would place his hand over my mouth and say, "Shut up!" Milton remembers walking into my room one night and my stepfather telling him to leave. Amazed that he remembered, Milton said, "for some reason I have an image of your eyes wide open with his hands over your mouth etched in my brain. I always wondered why that image never left me."

My mother and stepfather owned a locksmith and record business when we were in elementary school. Strangely, the building where those businesses were housed, were located directly across the street from our school. Often we would leave school and stop by the record store. I have many memories of that building. I confided in Milton that our stepfather would insist that I stop by the business after school where I was molested in the back of the building or in the back room.

He would literally pull me off the street and violate me in the company van. I shared with my brother so many stories about the abuse I endured, that he ran out of the house screaming. He couldn't believe that all I wanted to do was sleep in his bed hoping it would stop. My brother said, "No!" I told him of the times I sought help from the neighbors, but the neighbors said, "I was too fast" and that they were staying out of it. I befriended several girls in the neighborhood and tried to spend as much time as possible with them. Their parents grew weary of my presence and would send me home. No one could imagine what I was thinking as I walked home, thinking of what would happen to me at night.

Milton couldn't wait for our mother to return so that he could tell her what happened. Once she arrived, we were sitting in the kitchen and he asked her to sit with us. Milton began to tell our mother all that happened and for some reason, he didn't think that she was too surprised. After hearing Milton and myself, my mother called my grandmother and told her what happened, but again I don't think she was too surprised either. Something had to be done.

The police was called and my stepfather was arrested and charged. Sometime later we were all called into court to testify as to what we knew. Since our older siblings were not living in the house during this time, there wasn't much they could say, so Milton's testimony was needed. He remembered being the age of twelve or so sitting on the witness stand telling all that he knew. When he was finished the judge dismissed him and instructed him to wait in the hallway. At the close of the hearing I recall fainting in the lobby of the courthouse. My sister Jackie held onto me to prevent me from falling, at the same time punching the walls in the corridor. When Milton asked Jackie what happened, she replied in her colorful language, "that — got off." What happened in the courtroom traumatized our family for years to come. I went to live with different members of my family.

Milton and my mother moved out of the house and into an apartment. As a result of the outcome of the trial, I was taken to live with my sister in Austin, Texas. Mother moved back in with my stepfather and they continued to live together. No one talked about me being abused anymore. We all went on living as if nothing happened.

Silence didn't mean all was well. I harbored hatred in my heart toward my mother and stepfather for years. The hurt and pain carried over into my adult life and abusive behavior continued with my children, family, and friends.

I must say, in revealing the things I have experienced, it is not meant to degrade my parents. Through God's grace He has enabled me to forgive and restore our relationship. This story is to help and encourage others who were abused.

6

My Damascus Road

A Peek Inside

"The greatest tragedy in life is not death, but a life without a purpose." Dr. Myles Munroe

As I open the curtains to my life approximately 12 years ago I began to see everything I am and everything I'm not. In my perspective, I was holding on and doing the best I could. I was just breathing and functioning.

During that season in life, I was married to my third husband and caring for two young children. Pretty much every one that I befriended knew there was something peculiar about me. My house had to be immaculate, the children always kept impeccably neat, and I demanded what I wanted. There were some deep underlying issues in my life, however, I still managed to love and care for people. On the flip side of that, I could be so mean, cold, and hurtful. Throughout the years of disappointment and abuse I had become callous to feeling anything.

Many friends didn't know the depth of my pain. I began to share my life with a few people who became my close friends and whom I dared to trust. I revealed the horrendous acts of childhood abuse from my stepfather, various people saying, "She's going to end up dead", fighting every day, and constantly getting a beating by my mother. It's hard finding words to express how I felt to have all this swept under the rug and be told that you're going to be ok. I guess "angry" will suffice for now.

I endured many disappointments and heart aches in my adult life. My second marriage ended in divorce and separation from five of my children. At that time it was the best decision on behalf of the children. Their father was awarded custody due to the life I was living and the choices that I made. The children were disciplined harshly, almost as bad as the treatment that I received from my mother. They couldn't sit on certain furniture and bedrooms had to be perfect or there would be no play time or disciplinary action. Their dad, who was a military officer, did an outstanding job in rearing them along with me. I must say, "at that time he was the best dad any child would love to have and a friend you could trust."

Throughout the years, I longed to be a part of my children's lives, but our family was shattered. It became broken and seemed irreparable.

While broken on the inside, I made the decision to move on with life, trying to love everyone the best I knew how. Filled with anger, it didn't take much for me to lash out at anyone who I felt did something offensive to me. I could have severed many friendships, but I was told that they held onto the good in me, the fun moments, laughter, love, and energy I contributed to their lives.

I learned to mask any signs of pain and hurt very well. At times, anger would flare up when I was offended, but majority of the time, nobody could tell if I was bothered by anything. Responses given after the offenses were mostly unsuspected. I would get you back with a vengeance and you would be blown away. I didn't have to physically hurt anyone; it was a matter of using words that would cut. If someone disrespected me, I had a way of taking care of it, and making sure that it didn't happen again. I met a few people in the parking lot of the church and showed them a side of me they hadn't seen before. A bomb dropped on them that made their heads spin. You see I wasn't so holy that I couldn't lay you out. Sometimes my closest friends wondered why were they still my friend because they could get the same treatment as well. Sometimes they did.

Throughout all of this, there was a place deep inside that could still love. I loved when people didn't love me back. I loved when people in the dance ministry talked about me and put me out of the ministry. I loved when my daughter was put out of the dance ministry. Yet, some of these same people, I gave beautiful gifts to on several occasions and didn't get anything in return, nor did I expect anything. I loved through the hurt. Rejected by my mother, rejected by people, I never gave up on God or going to church because that is all I had to hold onto for comfort. My life was in shambles and I was headed down the road of destruction.

The life I was living caused me to end up in courtrooms, police stations, and hospitals. Things couldn't get any worse and I had to change my lifestyle or self-destruct. I called on the name of Jesus and He met me where I was, on my Damascus Road. I surrendered to God once and for all and allowed the power of the Holy Spirit to transform my life.

Being committed to God, I stayed in His presence out of desperation for change. He called me out of the darkness in which I had lived for so long and brought me into His marvelous light. I began to heal from the inside out. My soul sings;

> *Everlasting, your light shines when all else fades,*
> *Never ending, your glory goes beyond all fame, and*
> *the cry of my heart is to give you praise from the*
> *inside out.*

As transformation and healing took place, the Lord began to show me that I needed to ask for forgiveness from many people that I hurt. He directed me to a friend from many years ago. I went to her home and knelt down outside, on my knees crying, I asked for forgiveness. Amazingly, she said, "I forgave you a long time ago and I still want to be your friend". I went to several other people also to make amends. The blessing is that they forgave with gladness in their heart.

I forgave my mother and stepfather for abusing me. This was a huge step in the process. I found that when you release people, God will release you and open doors more than you can think or imagine. The Lord Almighty, shut some doors and opened others.

When I was put out of the dance ministry, that event propelled me into my destiny. Glory to God! I founded True Worship Prophetic Ministry of Dance and Worshipping Arts and Bethel House of God Prayer Line. During this season, I also opened by heart and home to sisters in need of assistance and encouragement.

God was doing some miraculous things in my life and I began to wonder what was my calling and purpose in life. I remember distinctly asking the Lord in 2012, "Why did I have to go through that abuse as a little girl? Why me? Why am I here?" God answered in a soft audible voice, "People can see my Glory through you and your testimony. I made you for my Glory." What was meant for evil, God turned around for my good. "Your latter shall be greater." said the Lord.

I have walked on the Damascus Road and now abide under the shadow of the Almighty, who is my refuge and my fortress. I was *broken, but not destroyed* and God gave me beauty for ashes. Thank you Yeshua that the cycle of abuse is broken in my family's life and I will continue to confess the compassion of Christ as surely as the Lord lives, to everyone.

7

The Healing Process

"You can suffer the pain of change or suffer remaining the way you are." Joyce Meyer

The point of this book is to help those who have been abused. It's to let you know that you don't have to stay in a stuck place. You don't have to be bent over for the rest of your life. I shared my story and you read an inside glimpse of what it was like to be in Mavis' world. I needed healing and if you have had any trauma in your life, you need healing too. We can be set free and no longer bound in the chains of the past. Are you ready to be free? Then allow the Lord to go into the secret place hidden in your heart that no one has ever entered. Let God in and trust Him with you (your heart, mind, and soul) so that the healing process can begin.

    The healing process won't be completed overnight. If you have been bound emotionally and spiritually for any number of years, it's going to take some time to undo bad behaviors and replace them with godly behaviors. Trust God and know that perfect love casts out fear (1 John 4:18). Be willing to open your heart before the Lord and drop your defenses. Let down that ten foot wall you have built over the years. You can't go into the process with fear if you desire to be free. Strip yourself of your own thought process and do it God's way. His way is the only way. Isaiah 55: 6-9 *Seek ye the Lord while he may be found, call ye upon him while he is near: 7 Let the wicked forsake his way, and the unrighteous man his thoughts: and let him return unto the Lord, and he will have mercy upon him; and to our God, for he will abundantly pardon. 8 For my thoughts are not your thoughts, neither are your ways my ways, saith the Lord. 9 For as the heavens are higher than the earth, so are my ways higher than your ways, and my thoughts than your thoughts.* **Point One: Seek God, Call on Him, turn to the Lord.**

In working towards healing, put selfishness, low self-esteem, and pride under your feet and allow God love you. Only God can love perfectly without fault. No matter how much man tries to love you, it impossible for it to be perfect because we are human. Humans are born into the world with a sinful nature, subject to mistakes, and fall short of another's expectations. In Matthew 26:41 the Word says, *"the spirit indeed is willing, but the flesh is we*ak."

I had a bad habit of trying to get a piece of love from everybody. One friend could provide this, another friend could provide that, and this friend is good at this. God's love was nowhere in those friendships and relationships. Stop looking for love in all of the wrong places and things that make you feel good temporarily. Your only source is God and He is the root of love in you.

Accept God's love by being conscious of it and by putting your faith in it (1John 4: 16). When one accepts the fact that God loves them regardless of what they have gone through or have done, he doesn't have to look for acceptance through people. I did that for years. I wanted acceptance by having all of the latest fashions, most recent CD's for music, hair styled every week, and nails and toes perfectly groomed just so that people would see me in a grand way. I didn't want to give room for anyone to say anything about me but good which covered any worthless feeling that resided on the inside. Don't wait for someone to make you feel good about you, because when they fail, you will be hurt again and the walls will go up again. I learned to get past putting on the masks of the outer appearance by acknowledging that God really loves me and has a plan for me. **Point Two: Stop expecting people to give you what only God can provide. Stop looking for temporary fixes, and love yourself.** Accept God's unconditional love. He knows all that you have been through and He has been right there with you all the way.

Spiritual House Cleaning

The process of healing disease, sickness, and sin resulting from abusive behavior involved sitting at the Lord's feet constantly and removing myself from ungodly living. Anything that was made an idol in my life (things and people) had to be removed. All things that were tainted with sin in my living space had to be removed. Every item that was given to me through ungodly relationships had to be discarded (cards, clothes, rings, jewelry, furniture). I had to make a choice. It was time for spiritual house cleaning to bring Godly order in my life. Making the genuine choice to give God first place in my life, meant letting go of a false sense of security that I hung onto through people. I found security in God, not man (Psalm 40:2 *He lifted me out of the slimy pit, out of the mud and mire; he set my feet on a rock and gave me a firm place to stand*). This only happened after I chose to put God first (Exodus 20:3 *"You shall have no other gods before me."*) **Point Three: Anything not of God's character, put it under your feet and rebuke it in the name of Jesus. Get rid of contamination.**

The Holy Spirit spoke to me and gave instructions to clean house *physically and spiritually*.

I had to gut out the old me and allow God to renew a pure and right spirit in my heart (Psalm 51:10 Create in me a pure heart, O God, and renew a steadfast spirit within me.)

Here are some ways to start cleaning your house for God:

1. **Identify strongholds both positive and negative in your heart.** A stronghold is either negative or positive, *a lie* or *truth*. Whatever thought a person chooses to accept or receive, own or possess, rely or depend on, protect or defend and act upon is a stronghold in that person's life whether it is a lie or the truth. A stronghold is also a demonic fortress of thought housing evil spirits that control, dictate, and influence your attitude and behavior. It oppresses and discourages you. They are inspired by satan. When you think on them, your emotions become attached to them. Then you act on it and once a habit is developed, it is a stronghold. Strongholds also color

and filter how we view the world and control how we react to situations.

If we entertain ungodly thoughts and participate in activities that are contrary to the will of God, we open ourselves to demonic habitation in those areas. We become immune to evil around us and we cannot hear God's voice as clear and loud as we once did. The chief goal of the enemy is to destroy our intimate relationship with the Father, Jesus, the Holy Spirit, and with those in our household. These are the targets the devil seeks to destroy. He wants us to become emotionally isolated from God.

Anything that you have dealt with in your past, as a believer in Christ run the other way. Don't let your guard down. The enemy could be setting you up for a fall. Every stronghold that you break off your life, you also break off of your generation and your children.

2. **Walk through your home and remove every object that may have a demonic attachment.** Example: clothes, magazines, music, posters, CD's, DVD's, pictures (all ungodly relationships), movies (rated R and pornography), statues or figurines (ex. Buddha's). Make sure demonic items brought in the home doesn't bring spiritual interference. Take a spiritual inventory of the home and yourself.

3. **Listen to the voice of God more clearly** to be able to move forth when He tells you to do His will.

4. **Renounce/ remove negative strongholds to walk in spiritual freedom.** 2 Corinthians 10:3-6 *For though we live in the world, we do not wage war as the world does. 4 The weapons we fight with are not the weapons of the world. On the contrary, they have divine power to demolish strongholds. 5 We demolish arguments and every pretension that sets itself up against the knowledge of God, and we take captive every thought to make it obedient to Christ. 6 And we will be ready to punish every act of disobedience, once your obedience is complete.*

As soon as a negative thought enters the mind, cast it down, don't entertain it. God wants our home to be a place where He dwells.

The Healing Process

If you willingly contaminate your home and yourself with unclean things, God will allow destruction for you and your family.

Look at Joshua 6: 18-19 *But keep away from the devoted things, so that you will not bring about your own destruction by taking any of them. Otherwise you will make the camp of Israel liable to destruction and bring trouble on it. 19 All the silver and gold and the articles of bronze and iron are sacred to the Lord and must go into his treasury." Joshua 7:1 But the Israelites were unfaithful in regard to the devoted things; Achan son of Karmi, the son of Zimri,[b] the son of Zerah, of the tribe of Judah, took some of them. So the Lord's anger burned against Israel.*

Joshua 7:10-12 *The Lord said to Joshua, "Stand up! What are you doing down on your face? 11 Israel has sinned; they have violated my covenant, which I commanded them to keep. They have taken some of the devoted things; they have stolen, they have lied, they have put them with their own possessions. 12 That is why the Israelites cannot stand against their enemies; they turn their backs and run because they have been made liable to destruction. I will not be with you anymore unless you destroy whatever among you is devoted to destruction.*

Now look at what the Lord says in verse 13

"Go, consecrate the people. Tell them, 'Consecrate yourselves in preparation for tomorrow; for this is what the Lord, the God of Israel, says: There are devoted(unclean) things among you, Israel. You cannot stand against your enemies until you remove them.

5. **Remove anything unclean right now, this very moment**. Do not ignore strongholds. They come in many forms and some ways you may not expect or have not thought about.

Examine yourself and see if you need to address:
Pride
Religiosity
Independence & divorce
Insensitivity (unaware of your impact on others, ignore others views)
Impatient (don't tolerate other people delays)
Rebellion (self-will, full of strife)

Fear and insecurity (inferiority, inadequate)
Timidity (shyness, bashfulness, making wrong decisions to fit in)
Perfectionist
Dread of failure
Inability to set goals
Sexual impurity (sex outside of marriage, masturbation, pornography, fantasy)

Now that you have identified physical and spiritual strongholds in your life, you need to know how to remove them permanently. We do that by going to the Word of God. You need to replace areas of darkness and flood it with prayer, faith, love, scripture, meditation, church, Bible study, study groups, and an accountability partner.

When tempted, choose the Word of God. *Psalm 34:17-19 The righteous cry out, and the Lord hears them; he delivers them from all their troubles. 18 The Lord is close to the brokenhearted and saves those who are crushed in spirit. 19 The righteous person may have many troubles, but the Lord delivers him from them all.*

We are to follow Jesus' example when we struggle with a stronghold in our minds. When Satan reminds of us of past sin or past hurt we are to remember the Word and speak it. Jesus was not using His power as God, but was acting as man and in a weakened condition. When Satan came to Him, Christ used the Word as a sword and quickly rebuked the Devil. We use the Word as a sword to fight the battle.

1 Corinthians 10:13 No temptation has overtaken you except what is common to mankind. And God is faithful; he will not let you be tempted beyond what you can bear. But when you are tempted, he will also provide a way out so that you can endure it.

Change your thinking to God's way of thinking. Know your position in Christ, you have authority. Matthew 16:19 *"I will give you the keys to the kingdom of heaven. Whatever you bind on earth shall be bound in heaven; and whatever you loose on earth shall be loosed in heaven."*

John 14:13-14
13 "You can ask for anything in my name, and I will do it, because the work of the Son brings glory to the Father. 14 Yes, ask anything in my name, and I will do it!"

Keep fighting and don't give up. *Matthew 7:7-8 "Keep on asking, and you will be given what you ask for. Keep on looking, and you will find. Keep on knocking, and the door will be opened. 8 For everyone who asks, receives. Everyone who seeks, finds. And the door is opened to everyone who knocks.*

Do not give up! Whatever it is that you are trying to overcome, will be defeated. The victory is your; Christ has given it to you. Each time you come up against it, walls break down and keep breaking down until the barrier in your mind is gone and Satan does not have easy access to make you feel unworthy or unloved. Trust in the Lord with all your heart and do not lean to your own understanding!

When you fight your battle on your knees, you win every time. We must have clean hands and a pure heart before the Lord.

Understanding Curses

Curses don't come without a cause. Someone, somewhere, sometime, committed a sin or sins against God and that opened up a "legal door" or reason for the curse. A curse is God's recompense (reward for wrongdoing) or repay. Unfortunately, the repayment comes in on your generations. Exodus 20:5 says that God is a jealous God and He is punishing the children for the sins of the parents to the third and fourth generations. Therefore, understand that any curse that you have been living under comes from the sins committed by previous generations. I ask you to take a look at the women or men in your family. Do you see any noticeable patterns of iniquity? Do you see perversion, mischief, moral evil, loss of virginity, abortions, etc.? The pattern of perversion is the cause of the curse.

Perversion is doing the wrong thing; turning away from what is good or morally right. Some of the patterns you won't know until you sit and speak with members of your family to find out traits and characteristics of others.

You may find sexual perversion, financial trouble, shop-a-holic, religious, worshipping idols, occult, sorcery, behavioral issues, poverty, speaking idle words like "I'm so stupid", or controlling spirits. When you recognize any patterns in your family, do you fit in it? There's a great chance that you do. Generational curses are very real and it passed down to you.

When you read about my life in Chapter 5, one can see that abuse, fighting, hatred, and abandonment was passed on to me from my grandmother and my mother. I was about to transfer the same curse to my children. I loved them dearly; however, when it was time for discipline, I whipped them harshly, was mean, and very controlling.

The great news in my life and yours is that the curse can be broken. Once you know that you have lived under a curse, you can stop it right now. The Bible says in Galatians 3:13-14 *Christ redeemed us from the curse of the law by becoming a curse for us, for it is written: "Cursed is everyone who is hung on a pole." 14 He redeemed us in order that the blessing given to Abraham might come to the Gentiles through Christ Jesus, so that by faith we might receive the promise of the Spirit.* Begin to speak the Word of God out of your mouth to release the blessings in your life. Now that you know, break the cycle for you and your children and the generations to come.

1. Repent for the generations that sinned and repent for you. Renounce completely–Renounce means to totally give up, And refuse to commit the sin again in Jesus' name. Ask God for forgiveness based on the Blood of Jesus for my ancestors actions and attitudes, as well as my own.

    Leviticus 26:40 *But if they confess their iniquity and the iniquity of their fathers in their treachery that they committed against me, and also in walking contrary to me, 41 so that I walked contrary to them and brought them into the land of their enemies—if then their uncircumcised heart is humbled and they make amends for their iniquity, 42 then I will remember my covenant with Jacob, and I will remember my covenant with Isaac and my covenant with Abraham, and I will remember the land.*

2. Ask God to help me no longer agree with or do that sin.
3. Remember that once the curse is broken, we must continue in God to keep it broken. Also, we need to remember that God wants us to be free and He is always willing to break a curse. Like everything else, we have to do our part for Him to do His part.
4. Realize that what we do affects our children and our grandchildren.

Pray out loud this powerful prayer to break the chain of strongholds and generational curses off of you and your family.

*Father God, in the mighty name of Jesus, I thank you every day for keeping me. You are truly my Jehovah Shalom, my peace, the peace that surpasses all understanding. You are the Lord, my Great Lord, El Adonai, who has total authority. You are El Roi, the God who sees me and knows all about me. You Lord, are El Shaddai, God Almighty, and my problems are not too big for you to handle. You are Jehovah Rapha, the Lord who heals. You are the cure for spiritual, physical, and emotional sickness through Jesus Christ. God you know my beginning and my end. You know all that I have endured and what my family has endured. But I thank God you lifted up a standard, first in Jesus, and then in your son/daughter (**say your name here**). Because I know that I have the authority in Jesus to cast out demons and put the enemy under my feet, I speak boldly today to break every generational curse made known to me by the power of the Holy Spirit.*

*God, my great God, as I stand in the gap, I confess the sins and iniquities of my ancestors through the (**say the name of your families on both sides**) pride, alcohol, drugs, prostitution, fornication, sexual sins, homosexuality, molestation, arrogance, abandonment, voodoo and witchcraft emotional abuse, control, physical abuse, stealing, greed, and impatience (**include your family sins and iniquities**).*

Lord, forgive everyone one in my family bloodline and me for operating in sin and iniquity. No more passing the buck, it stops here and it stops now! The chains are broken and will not spring up in my children or their children, or any children to come.

God in the powerful name of Jesus, I cast out the demon of lust, hate, pride, lying, deceit, hoarding, haste, jealousy, envy, gossiping, and malicious behavior. They are under my feet and I step on and crack the neck of the enemy and destroy every attack from the root! I break the enemies head, back, arm, hand and foot, and every crack or crevice that was open is now closed. I renounce and denounce any part of it trying to linger or hang around my family. Get out of here!

Father God, I thank you for redeeming me and my children from the curse. For the law of the spirit, of life in Christ Jesus has set me free from the law of sin and death. There is therefore no condemnation to me or my family in Christ Jesus! The curse is broken. God I ask you to fill my family with you in every place of our lives. Fill the emotional abuse with your Compassion; fill impatience with Fasting and Prayer; fill hoarding with Giving, fill envy with Love, fill lust with Desire for You (Yeshua), fill pride with Humbleness; fill lying with the Truth, fill hastiness and foolishness with Wisdom, fill gossiping with the Word. Fill us Oh Lord until the very fibers of our being exudes you, Father.

Thank you for destroying bondage at the root Lord. My life and my children's lives shall be blessed and overflowing in fruitfulness. In Jesus' name, Amen!

8

Pivotal Points

"When you focus on being a blessing, God makes sure that you are always blessed in abundance."
Joel Osteen

There are some pivotal points to keep in mind as you go through emotional healing. God has always shown believers from the beginning of the Bible to the end of the Bible His faithfulness and loyalty. The Lord is immutable and He never changes. We are the ones that have to hold onto faith in Christ and not doubt or waiver. If the Father said He will never leave you or forsake you, then we must trust His Word.

Let's look at Hosea and Gomer in the Book of Hosea. Hosea suffered much because his wife Gomer was an adulterer. Yet he remained faithful to her out of obedience to God. Eventually, Gomer has a situation where she is being sold to the highest bidder. Hosea, who loves her, comes to her rescue and buys her back. This is an illustration of God's love for Israel and how he leaves room for hope and reconciliation. As you heal, God yearns for you to love Him just as much as He loves you. *The Lord is faithful and He won't turn His back on you.*

(Isaiah 55:11 so is my word that goes out from my mouth: It will not return to me empty, but will accomplish what I desire.)

In Genesis chapter 25, Jacob stole the birthright from his twin brother Esau. Esau was so angry with Jacob that he wanted to kill him, so Jacob fled. The years the brothers spent apart, they married and had children. Jacob who had obtained the blessings from their father, Isaac, birthed the Twelve Tribes of Israel. By the time Jacob traveled to go back home, time had healed Esau's wound. Their reunion was one of forgiveness and restoration. If you have been wounded and scarred like Esau, God can restore you back to your original state of happiness and peace. You don't have to stay wounded forever. *Forgive so that God's love and peace can reign in your life and any burdens you were carrying can be lifted.* (Matthew 30:11 For my yoke is easy and my burden is light.")

We also learn valuable teaching from looking at Ezekiel, the prophet. Ezekiel's purpose was to announce judgment on Israel and other nations for their sins. God told Ezekiel that Israel won't listen to you because they are not willing to listen to me. Israel was a rebellious people whose heart was hardened. However, the Lord says in Chapter 3:8, that He will make Ezekiel harder than they are. He will make Ezekiel's forehead like the hardest stone. The Lord instructs Ezekiel to go to those who are exiled in Babylon and speak to them without fear. Then the Spirit lifted Ezekiel and took him away in bitterness and an angry spirit with the hand of the Lord on Him.

The critical lesson to draw from this is that, God placed on the inside of Ezekiel the tools necessary to carry out His instructions. God equipped him to accomplish the assignment that was given and made him accountable to obey. Ezekiel had to be more hardened to be able to stand in Israel's face and declare what God said. Therefore, God has already placed everything on the inside of you as well. You may not be specifically sent to a group of people to speak, but you should be as angry about sin as Ezekiel was when it comes to your personal life.

You are accountable to stand against unforgiveness, bitterness, gossip, and other sins. *It's your responsibility to trust God.* When you live the way God wants you to live and obey his commands and decrees, he promises to restore you. Though you were abandoned, broken, or bruised, He says;

I will sprinkle clean water on you, and you will be clean,
I will cleanse you from all impurities and from your idols,
I will give you a new heart and put a new spirit in you,

I will remove from you a heart of stone and give you a heart of flesh. (Ezekiel 36:24-26)

An essential reason why we have to live a life of being grateful, thankful, and appreciative in life can be found in Romans chapter 9. The Apostle Paul gives a clear understanding to some of the questions most believers and non-believers have regarding why things happen to them.

First, God's Word does not fail. His plan will be completed whether He uses you or someone else to get it done. There is a purpose for everything. Verse 14 asks, "Is God unjust?" The answer that follows is, "Not at all!" Because he told Moses, "I will have mercy on whom I have mercy and I will have compassion on whom I have compassion." This is God's sovereign choice. He also hardens who He wants to harden. Then the question is, "why does God still blame us?" Paul states, "Who are we to talk back to God? Who are we to ask why did you make me this way? Or why did that happen to me?" Here the simple biblical answer. God has the right to make whomever He will for great purposes, some for common use, and even some for destruction. Why? Look at Romans 9:17. God raised up Pharaoh in Exodus 9:16 so that he could be used to declare God's power. God used him to show salvation was God's proper work, not mans. The Creator has control over the created object. Judas, one of the twelve disciples was used. He was used for betrayal, and then hung himself. His purpose was over.

Everything that has happened in your life was for a reason. God wants you to realize your very existence depends on Him. We can only be saved by putting our trust in what Jesus has done. If we do that we will never be put to shame or disappointed.

9

Finishing the Race

Stand Firm

I learned that if I didn't commit to achieving my own happiness, no one else would. Brian Tracy

I would love to say that my transformation of beauty for ashes was a piece of cake. However, anything worth achieving takes hard work and effort.

After my process of house cleaning, breaking strongholds and curses, I began to work towards being stronger in Christ to maintain my deliverance and freedom from bondage. One of the ways I did this was to exercise spiritual disciplines. As I woke up every morning, I purposed prayer and quality time with the Lord. My motto became "Take God everywhere I go." No longer would I allow myself to disrespect the Lord by conveniently pushing Him to the side and picking Him back up when I felt like it. When I purposed God in my life, it kept me from falling into snares and entrapments (2 Timothy 2: 26 *and that they will come to their senses and escape from the trap of the devil, who has taken them captive to do his will.*) I literally hid myself in Christ to stop doing familiar things and going to familiar places (Psalm 91 *Whoever dwells in the shelter of the Most High will rest in the shadow of the Almighty. 2 I will say of the Lord, "He is my refuge and my fortress, my God, in whom I trust.).*

There were many darts thrown by the devil and demons to distract me. People that could have tempted me to backslide called constantly, offered money and gifts, and invitations to dinner. Some on several occasions tried to enter into my sacred place of prayer. However, every time I denied satan access into my life I grew stronger and wiser. Strength, patience, and trust in God prevailed. I literally fed myself the Word all day to renew my mind to the things of God (Romans 12:2 *Do not be conformed to this world, but be transformed by the renewal of your mind, that by testing you may discern what is the will of God, what is good and acceptable and perfect.* I barricaded myself in the basement for months to stay away from people and temptation. A fresh start and new beginning was taking place. I wouldn't say that I didn't fall short sometimes, because I did.

However, I got up, repented, and looked to the hills from where my help comes. My help comes from the Lord.

My dwelling space with God was limited to family only. It was sacred and I couldn't have the stench of sin from past relationships or unholy conversation in God's Holy habitation. I set up a tabernacle (physical tabernacle) in my prayer room. I hung banners expressing praise and worship to God (John 4:24-26 *God is a Spirit: and they that worship him must worship him in spirit and in truth.*

The only shows allowed on television were Christian movies and Christian television. I wanted so much to be changed from who I used to be. Modification of my clothes for church and events outside of church changed to modest apparel. I allowed the Holy Spirit dress me every morning. Most times if the clothes I chose for the day were too flamboyant, the Holy Spirit would tell me to change it. My new mindset was to live a life of humility, trust, love, faith, obedience, and perseverance.

Close friends thought the changes were too drastic. They waited for me to change back to the old me any day (Galatians 5:17 *For the flesh lusteth against the Spirit, and the Spirit against the flesh: and these are contrary the one to the other: so that ye cannot do the things that ye would.*) But I stood firm in the choice to take up my cross and follow Christ (Matthew 16:24-25 *Then Jesus said to his disciples, "Whoever wants to be my disciple must deny themselves and take up their cross and follow me. 25 For whoever wants to save their life will lose it, but whoever loses their life for me will find it.).*

In my prayer I would ask God to show me His face and He did. Times when I was in prayer and yearned for God, He would let me know He was there by showing me doves. I would cry almost every day because I realized how much he loved me and saved me from destruction. It took almost being destroyed for me to wake up and call on God. I was troubled emotionally, spiritually, and physically. I had done so much wrong, I was on my way to despair and destruction.

In one of the roughest times of my life, I set up a sanctuary for God. Choosing the Lord and choosing to live a life of holiness saved my life. Sacrifice and obedience, and Prayer and Faith became a lifestyle. Every step in the process of going to the next level is work. Don't look at how far you have to go, but instead look at how far you have come. Look at how God is restoring and healing, and enjoy the process. It's not a woe it's me time, but a time to enjoy the renewing of the mind. Allow God to take you from Glory to Glory (2 Corinthians 3:18 *But we all, with open face beholding as in a glass the glory of the Lord, are changed into the same image from glory to glory, even as by the Spirit of the Lord).*

Below is a list of common spiritual practices which many Christians have practiced throughout the centuries.

Bible Study	Service
Prayer	Solitude
Fasting	Discernment
Worship	Evangelism

Spiritual disciplines should be:
- Instruments of God's grace which, through the Spirit, transform us daily into people who reflect Jesus' love, obedience, humility, and connection to God.
- A source of humility and dependence on God.
- Practices that give us hope, despite our failings and limitations.
- Practices that permeate every area of our lives.

- Experiences that enrich our lives and the lives of those around us.
- Activities that connect us deeply to other believers in our common desire to follow God's will.

Spiritual disciplines should not be:
- Heavy loads of impossible, unrealistic, or unfair expectations of people.
- A way to hide our sins with good works.
- Benchmarks to judge people's Christianity or maturity.
- Individualistic attempts to be holy or perfect.

Spiritual disciplines help us get ready for difficult moments: moments of persecution, temptation, doubt, and grief.

10

Exercise Patience for the Promises

May the Warm Winds of Heaven
Blow softly upon your house.
May the Great Spirit
Bless all who enter there.
May your Mocassins
Make happy tracks
in many snows,
and may the Rainbow
Always touch your shoulder
Sun Bear

To be patient is to endure discomfort without complaint. This calls into play some other virtues, specifically, self-control, humility, and generosity. An example from the life of Christ illustrates this. Jesus was very patient with his disciples. They were sometimes thickheaded, lazy, selfish, and slow to believe. In spite of Jesus' miracles and words of wisdom, they were focused upon themselves and wavered in their belief about who he really was. To say that was uncomfortable for Jesus would be an understatement.

Notice that Jesus' refusal to complain about his irritating disciples can be described as an exercise of self-control. Also, his refusal to complain involves humility, the conscious decision to lower himself by not exercising his right, as the holy man he was, to judge and dismiss his friends because of their faults. Finally, Jesus' refusal to

Exercise Patience for the Promises

complain about his disciples is generous. In spite of their faults and thick-headedness, he remained no less committed to them and served them increasingly as their failures became more outstanding.

Jesus Christ, our greatest example, endured discomfort and irritation without complaining. This should be one of your main priorities in purposing to live a victorious life. In Christ we inherit the promises of God. If we know that God has already made provision for us to win, then make up your mind to do the work and God promises to get you through. Every step you take in renewing your mind is a faith walk and a decision to trust God no matter what circumstances look like. Give God your pain, so that you can live. Every time you see visions of your offender molesting, beating, tormenting, and abusing you give it to God and leave it there.

Every pain, hurt, anger, offense, or discomfort, turn it over to the Lord and live. You are not in that situation anymore; leave your baggage at the Altar and anticipate receiving the promises of God in your life.

Hebrews 10: 19-23*Therefore, brothers and sisters, since we have confidence to enter the Most Holy Place by the blood of Jesus, 20 by a new and living way opened for us through the curtain, that is, his body, 21 and since we have a great priest over the house of God, 22 let us draw near to God with a sincere heart and with the full assurance that faith brings, having our hearts sprinkled to cleanse us from a guilty conscience and having our bodies washed with pure water. 23 Let us hold unswervingly to the hope we profess, for he who promised is faithful.*

Be patient with yourself. There will be times when you may fall short or experience delay of progress. Delay does not mean failure or that God has left you. Everything that God does, He does it in His timing, not ours. The Lord knows what we need and when we need it. Start looking at delay as God giving you an opportunity to exercise your faith and patience. Continue to stand on the Word of God and do not quit (Galatians 6:9*And let us not grow weary of doing good, for in due season we will reap, if we do not give up*). God did not create weak sons and daughters, but children of might and strength. People will notice a change in you, stand firm. Some will try to bring up your past, stand because that's not who you are now. You have decided to lay down your burdens, cares, issues, and pain to follow Christ: You are redeemed by the blood of the Lamb. God said, "He will remember your sins no more (Hebrews 8:12)." You were given the opportunity to start living with a renewed mind and a right spirit. Romans 10:11 says, "Anyone who believe in Him (Jesus) will never be put to shame." Trust God in everything.

Persevere through the process to receive what God has promised. Hebrews 10: 32-34 *Remember those earlier days after you had received the light, when you endured in a great conflict full of suffering. 33 Sometimes you were publicly exposed to insult and persecution; at other times you stood side by side with those who were so treated. 34 You suffered along with those in prison and joyfully accepted the confiscation of your property, because you knew that you yourselves had better and lasting possessions.* The lasting possessions are everything that you obtain through Christ Jesus. No earthly thing can be compared to God's eternal things. The value of earthly possessions depreciates over time. The appearance becomes dull and tarnished, losing its luster and beauty. But, the value of God's possession increases over time as you live in Him through Christ. Everything that's the Lord is excellent, peaceful, joyful, illuminating, refreshing, eternal, and complete.

You are an heir to the promises and blessings that are His (Romans 8:17 And *if we are His children, then we are His heirs also: heirs of God and fellow heirs with Christ [sharing His inheritance with Him]; only we must share His suffering if we are to share His glory*). Persevere because it all belongs to you.

Put on the full armour of God every day. Every day you are in battle until the victory is won. Have your sword (the Word of God) by your side morning, noon, and night so when the enemy comes at your front, left, back, or right side, your armour is ready. Persevere because the enemy does not play fair. Jesus suffered and sacrificed before he experienced victory and you will also. If you can be patient through your process, you will experience God's abundant love and tender mercies.

Hebrews 10:35-37 *So do not throw away your confidence; it will be richly rewarded. 36 You need to persevere so that when you have done the will of God, you will receive what he has promised. 37 For, "In just a little while, he who is coming will come and will not delay.*

The reward of patience is the Promise. 2 Corinthians 1:20-22 *For no matter how many promises God has made, they are "Yes" in Christ. And so through him the "Amen" is spoken by us to the glory of God. 21 Now it is God who makes both us and you stand firm in Christ. He anointed us, 22 set his seal of ownership on us, and put his Spirit in our hearts as a deposit, guaranteeing what is to come.* Praise the Lord! He set his seal of ownership on us, gave us His spirit, guaranteeing that you will get what He promised. Leave your old torn up, dirty baggage and broken spirit at the altar and pick up your eternal blessings from heaven.

God is the only one who fortifies us to stand strong and unmovable in Christ. With His anointing and His Spirit in our hearts, you and I are guaranteed blessings. The prerequisite of the blessings and promises is having faith. Romans 4:16 *Therefore, the promise comes by faith, so that it may be by grace and may be guaranteed to all Abraham's offspring—not only to those who are of the law but also to those who have the faith of Abraham. He is the father of us all.*

What is said about God's promises to us?

7 Promises of God to Man

1. "But my God shall supply all your need according to his riches in glory by Christ Jesus". That's Phillipians 4:19. This includes food, clothing, shelter, companionship, love, and salvation thru Jesus Christ.
2. God has promised that His grace is sufficient for us. It is through an obedient faith that we have access into the grace of God according to Romans 5:2.
3. God has promised that His children will not be overtaken with temptation. Instead, He assures us that a way of escape will be provided. This promise is recorded in I Corinthians 10:13.
4. God has promised us victory over death. Peter said: "This Jesus hath God raised up, whereof we are all witnesses" (Acts 2:32).

5. God has promised that all things work together for good to those who love and serve Him faithfully (Romans 8:28).
6. God has promised that those who believe in Jesus and are baptized for the forgiveness of sins will be saved. (Mark 16:16 and Acts 2:38).
7. God has promised His people eternal life (John 10:27, 28).

11

Forgive Your Abusers

"Unforgiveness denies the victim the possibility of parole and leaves them stuck in the prison of what was, incarcerating them in their trauma and relinquishing the chance to escape beyond the pain." T.D. Jakes

Many people that have been abused find it hard to forgive their abusers. I walked around for years not forgiving my mother and my stepfather. There was so much I could hold against them how could I just let it go? I was living my life, working in all kinds of ministries in the church, yet harboring unforgiveness in my heart. For years I couldn't say, "I love you mother" and I hated when my stepfather was around. I wanted to turn from every kind of sin but that one, unforgiveness. It's a sin that's not easy to shake off because you feel like the abuser got away with hurting you. How can I love someone who didn't love me? They took my childhood and innocence away. Why did I have to grow up so fast and have embedded in my mind (for the rest of my life) those horrible things that happened to me? How do I forgive? It's much easier to say the word forgive, than it is to do it.

Let's take a step by step journey in the process of emotional healing that leads to being able to forgive. It's not possible to have good emotional health while harboring unforgiveness, resentment, and bitterness. The poison of this sin destroys and eats away at your inner being. You will die not your offender. Also it's impossible to get better and be bitter at the same time.

First, **you have a decision to make**. You can let each problem or hurt make you better or bitter. How can it make you a better person? Look at Romans 8:28 *And we know that in all things God works for the good of those who love him, who have been called according to his purpose.* God works in all things not just isolated incidents. Evil is all around us in this fallen world, but God is able to turn circumstances around for our long range good. God is working to fulfill His purpose and in the process you get the promise. However, this promise can be claimed only by those who love God and are called according to his purpose. Those who are called are those who the Holy Spirit convinces and enables to receive Christ. They have a new heart, mind, direction, and perspective. They trust God and look for their security in heaven, not on earth. They learn to accept the pain and not be resentful because God is with them.

My stepfather gave me away to my husband on my wedding day. Yes, he was my abuser, but I forgave him. Forgiveness does not depend on whether or not the person being forgiven deserves it. Forgiveness is a choice that is made as an act of obedience to God's Word.

Trust God and let Him fulfill his purpose. Only God has the power to change your feelings toward the person that abused you. God, through the power of the Holy Spirit, lives in you if you are born again. He alone can heal your inner man.

Satan intended on destroying you, but God can take whatever he plots against you and cause it to benefit you.

Secondly, *choose God's way of forgiveness*. It leads to a full victorious life as well as emotional health and healing. Even if you do not understand it, choose to follow it.

Thirdly, *learn about God's grace*. Grace is given to us freely although we have done nothing to earn it. It's the power of the Holy Spirit that comes to help us accomplish God's will. You have to extend grace to your offender.

In the book of James, the scripture said, "He gives more grace." He is referring to God. God give us more grace to humble ourselves, put pride aside along with hurt and anger. The Lord's grace will help you love and pray for your enemies (Matthew 5:44-45). It is important to remember while waiting for the Lord to move in someone else's life or your own, to keep doing what you know is the right (the Godly) thing to do.

When I genuinely started walking with the Lord, I began to pray for my mother. My stepfather had already passed away. Daily prayer started to change my perspective on all that I endured. No longer bitter with mother, I asked God to deliver, heal, and restore my mother in areas of her life. As I was praying for God to work in my mother's life, He also began to heal and restore my life, health, and well being. God's instruction for forgiving is written with detail in Luke 6: 27-28 *"But to you who are listening I say: Love your enemies, do good to those who hate you, 28 bless those who curse you, pray for those who mistreat you.* When you release your abusers from sins against you, God can bless your life. It is only in the strength of the Lord that this happens.

Last, when you choose to forgive [realizing that you cannot do it without God] *pray and release each person* who hurt you. It doesn't matter if you don't ever get an apology from your abuser, it's still important to forgive them. We must remember what Jesus Christ said on the cross, in agony and pain for things that were not his fault (Luke 23:34 "Father forgive them, for they know not what they do." This included the ones who laughed, scorned, and tormented him also.

Pray this prayer out loud:

Father God, your Word tells us that if we forgive those who have sinned against us, then You, our Heavenly Father, will forgive us. But, if we refuse to forgive others, You will not forgive us of our sins.

Today I choose to forgive. Father, I declare that I will be patient with people and forgive those who have offended me. I forgive_____ for_____, and I release them and let it go. Yahweh, forgive me for my sins. You said that if I confess my sins to You, You are faithful and just to forgive me and cleanse me from all wickedness. Therefore, Lord, please forgive me for _____. Help me Lord, and heal me of all the wounds inflicted upon me.

In Jesus' name, Amen.

Tame the Tongue
What You Speak Matters

An important step to take in forgiving your abuser is to stop talking about what was done. When in the midst of God-ordained counseling it may be necessary to mention it. In the midst of prayer for healing, it may be necessary. However, if you have been made free from unforgiveness, stop talking about the wrongdoing every time you speak with someone. Releasing your abuser means praying for them, not ruining their reputation. Letting go of those who have offended you means, not commenting anymore on the matter. The Bible teaches us not to slander, gossip, backbite, or spread rumors. Proverbs 20:19 says, *"A gossip betrays a confidence; so avoid anyone who talks too much."* In living a Christian life you should not gossip or slander.

Romans 1:29 also says, "They are gossip<u>s</u>". There are many forms of gossip and the Bible clearly says to stay away from those who do it.

I was a gossiper and slanderer before the Holy Spirit revealed to me what I was doing. Most times when I engaged in a conversation with people about the church I attended some years ago, I would talk about how the ministry leaders treated me, didn't like me, always put me in the back positions in dance ministry, and put me out of the ministry. But each day that I purposed the Lord in my life, the Holy Spirit would show me where I was wrong. The Holy Spirit gently said, "If you are free, then don't give a bad report (gossip) about this church and the members anymore. Leave them alone, it's over." It was a wakeup call to stop planting seeds (conversation that makes the listener question or assume something about the character of a person or group). God wants us to stop it because it is sin.

Turn those evil reports around and change your conversation. Here are some strategies to help resist gossip:
- You must purpose to guard your heart and be the bearer of good news.
- Be up front, and love those we talk about and talk to.
- Have a changed heart that loves God and loves people.

I never considered myself to be one of these and you probably didn't either, but there is a type of gossip called "spying". The Hebrew word translated as "gossip is *nakil* , which means a peddler of secrets, deceiver, or a spy. We might use the word "informer". The spy or informer descends on its prey like a military stealth bomber. A stealth bomber can fly undetected for quite a while and cannot be tracked easily. A spy will have a conversation with someone and he or she will never know that their words, expressions, actions, or gestures are being analyzed. The person won't catch what was going on until it done. The spy is one who wants to get the dirt on someone and then use that information to her or his advantage. The spy comes off as being trustworthy, but they really are not. They are motivated by hunger for power, enjoy making trouble, or just for the sake of knowing something that shouldn't be known. I wanted power. No more would I be trampled on by anyone and become the weaker vessel. After being mistreated and abused I made up my mind that I would be in control of me. I learned how to say certain words at the appropriate time to get things done my way. I use the power to include or exclude people and used what I knew about them to my advantage for revenge, payback, or self-gain. If you see yourself in this description, change your ways and motives. If it's not love, it's evil. The power of which you are really hungry for is Jesus. Jesus used his power to love and to be trustworthy so that we can entrust our deepest secrets to him knowing they are safe. You can learn to be trustworthy also.

The backstabber is another type of gossip. A backstabber is bent on revenge and retaliation. The backstabber desires for the target of her gossip to experience pain. They tell your shameful truths and smear your name with lies so that you hurt. This is the case where hurt people thrive on hurting other people. I was unhealthy and emotionally unstable for years. A lot of friends and family members were hurt by some of the things I said or did.

In the Bible, Absalom, was a backstabber. King David's son sat at the gates of Jerusalem and complained about his father's leadership (2 Samuel 15). He didn't say anything to David, but to all the people. Absalom wanted to steal the kingdom from King David. An example today is waiting for someone to die to get their money ("I can't wait for him to die, and then I will have money). This is hateful and sinful. Malicious gossip is the worst kind because it's most like satan's behavior (I hope he falls, I hope something happens to her). It tears apart people, and churches. However, backstabbers have to be aware. It often backfires. Proverbs 26:27-28 say, "If a man digs a pit, he will fall into it: if a man rolls a stone, it will roll back on him. The Gospel says to the backstabber, "Justice will be done. Leave it in the proper hands." Every wrong will be repaid at the cross or in the eternal judgment. Knowing this should change your heart and behavior. It changed mine.

The ways of the world seem right, but the Bible tells us in Romans 12:2 *Do not conform to the pattern of this world, but be transformed by the renewing of your mind. Then you will be able to test and approve what God's will is—his good, pleasing and perfect will.*

Jesus Christ died to set us free from sin. *"He himself bore our sins" in his body on the cross, so that we might die to sins and live for righteousness; "by his wounds you have been healed."*

Choose to love everyone because God is love. In loving people (including our abuser) we must be careful of the words we speak (James 3:9-10 *With the tongue we praise our Lord and Father, and with it we curse human beings, who have been made in God's likeness. 10 Out of the same mouth come praise and cursing. My brothers and sisters, this should not be.*

Line up your words with God's Word so that the words you speak can change your destiny. Unless revealing your problem has some Godly purpose, we must discipline ourselves to bear it silently, trusting that God will reward us openly for honoring His Word. If you truly forgive, resist gossip every day and speak Jesus. Flip the script on gossipers and surround yourself with people that have your same rhythm. Your conversations are true, honest, just, pure, lovely, and of a good report (Philippians 4:8).

Currently, my mother and I are on better speaking terms than ever before. Our conversations have grown to be pleasant, respectful, and accepting of prayer. On my last visit home, my mother cooked breakfast and dinner for me every day. We went shopping together and ended our evenings together. The highlight of the stay was that she actually spoke on True Worship Prophetic Ministry Prayer Line.

Our God is mighty and there is nothing too difficult for Him. Every day God is moving in her life in miraculous ways. I believe God has given my mother long life to witness the survival and accomplishments of my brother and me. We made it through the abuse and hardship and now live victoriously in Jesus Christ. We can live victoriously because we forgave. Yeshua has allowed us to see how wonderful life can be and what the devil meant for evil, God turned for our good. He will do the same for you.

12

Restoring Trust

Four keys to unlocking the heart…to replacing resentment with forgiveness, anger with understanding…to repairing the past with the possible… to rediscovering faith. -Max Lucado

Trust isn't an easy thing to do once it has been misused and abused. The very people that we were supposed to trust as children and young adults abused that trust.

Love for me wasn't really love, and gifts weren't really true gifts because most of the time there was a price to pay in receiving it. Therefore, walls and barriers were created in my heart that no one could cross. I kept it closed so no one would hurt that part of me anymore. It is possible that the greater the call on your life, the greater abuse that comes your way.

When disappointment would arise in a relationship, I could get out and move on to the next person. I would just move to the next person who could satisfy my need at that time. If that didn't last, I would move again to another friend. A circle of friends were created and each one met specific needs such as: help with children, lover, friend, cook, shop and entertainment, etcetera. I thought I had it going on as it seemed every type of person met a need or want. I just did a little bit of everything because I didn't trust relying on one person.

For many years, I put my trust in man rather than God. I relied on what man could do for me (which wasn't good because human feelings and emotions change). There were friends who were good to me but, still hurt me because people are not perfect *(Psalm 41:9 Even my close friend, someone I trusted, one who shared my bread,has turned against me)*. We did things and said words to each other that were hurtful which could have destroyed our friendship forever. The relevant message is; there is nothing wrong with having good friends, but instead of trusting them as your source, God Almighty has to be your only source. Good friendship is important, but so is balance.

When I decided to live for God, I chose to trust Him completely. Misplaced trust was restored back to the person it belonged to in the first place. *Proverbs 3:5-6 Trust in the Lord with all thine heart; and lean not unto thine own understanding. In all thy ways acknowledge him, and he shall direct thy paths.* The key points in this verse are to trust the Lord with all of you and acknowledging Him in everything. In other words, you believe that God will wake you up in the morning and allow rest at night. You believe that you will get to work safely.

There is belief that when you work, your employer will give you a paycheck. But is there belief that God can take your pain away? Can you lay hurt, bitterness, pain, fear, and anxiety at the feet of Jesus and leave it there? When you get on your knees to release it, God will be with you. He will take you step by step to a place you have yearned for a long time, freedom in Christ. Trusting the Lord with every fiber of your being, allows Him to restore Love, Faith, and Hope in you.

To maintain my trust in the Lord, I purpose to read Jeremiah 17:5-8: This is what the Lord says:

5"<u>Cursed is the one who trusts in man</u>,
who draws strength from mere flesh
and whose heart turns away from the Lord.
6 That person will be like a bush in the wastelands;
they will not see prosperity when it comes.
They will dwell in the parched places of the desert,
in a salt land where no one lives.
7"<u>But blessed is the one who trusts in the Lord</u>,
whose confidence is in him.
8 They will be like a tree planted by the water

that sends out its roots by the stream.
It does not fear when heat comes;
its leaves are always green.
It has no worries in a year of drought
and never fails to bear fruit."

There are two kinds of people in these verses, those who put their trust in man and those who trust in the Lord. The people who trust in man are unfruitful and the people who trust in the Lord will prosper. I choose the latter. When I trust in God, I know that everything is going to be alright. He is the life-giver, way-maker, and fruit bearer (producer of good) who keeps us planted firmly and supplies all our needs.

In choosing to trust God with your heart, He can now restore your broke places: image, health, strength, stability, peace, love, patience, perseverance, gentleness and faith. Your relationship with family and friends can be fully restored.

The Lord declares in Jeremiah 18:6 "…like clay in the hand of the potter so are you in my hand." Our God is capable of taking our brokenness and making us complete. Only Christ can rebuild what is broken and make it into something even better, but we must have faith that God can do that for us.

Be Thankful

One of the steps in restoration is being thankful. Thankfulness leads to trust- if you are thankful for what God's given you, then you will find it easy to trust Him in areas of your life. Look at all that Christ has done for you, it is impossible to feel rejected by your heavenly Father. God's Word actually commands us to be thankful: *Let the peace of Christ rule in your hearts, since as members of one body you were called to peace. And be thankful. (Colossians 3:15).*

Begin to be thankful for the little things which God has created for you to enjoy. Little things such as the birds singing in the trees, seeing beautiful rainbows, or feeling a cool breeze on your face – they were made for us to enjoy. When we realize what Christ has done for us, and are thankful for such an expensive gift that has been purchased with Jesus' own blood, then we will naturally forgive those who wrong us–that love is contagious and will flow through us. We cannot honestly look at what Christ has done for us, and not overflow with thankfulness in our heart. We must come to know the true good and loving nature of God towards His children.

Know that God is a great God and has your best interest in mind. He paves the way to being able to trust Him with the concerns in your life. You need to know that you can trust God with your needs, He understands them, and desires to help you! He really does look upon you with favor and hope! He's always calling us back to repentance, so that He can restore our relationship with Him.

Scriptures for meditation:

1 Thessalonians 5:18 Give thanks in all circumstances; for this is the will of God in Christ Jesus for you.

Psalm 107:1 Oh give thanks to the Lord, for he is good, for his steadfast love endures forever.

Jeremiah 30:17 For I will restore health to you, and your wounds I will heal, declares the Lord, because they have called you an outcast: 'It is Zion, for whom no one cares!'

Joel 2:25-26 I will restore to you the years that the swarming locust has eaten, the hopper, the destroyer, and the cutter, my great army, which I sent among you. "You shall eat in plenty and be satisfied, and praise the name of the Lord your God, who has dealt wondrously with you. And my people shall never again be put to shame.

Psalm 51:12 Restore to me the joy of your salvation, and uphold me with a willing spirit.

13

Fill My Cup

Lord, you alone are my portion and my cup; you make my lot secure. Psalm 16:5

In my life with Yeshua, I have everything I need. He is the meat and drink of my soul, supplies all of my necessities, my cup in this life, and my inheritance in the life to come. I am no longer empty and rejected, but filled with God's love and strength. No longer am I looking for something to make me feel good. I tried everything from satisfaction in jobs, promotions, church positions, friends, expensive brands of clothing, houses, social groups to join, and the desire for constant compliments. These are all the things that were to give me self-worth and let me know that I was acceptable and on my way to the top. I felt that way until I was delivered by God's Word through the Holy Spirit.

Joe – music

Chrystal –
46% off books

20 units
800-270-6951

Elle
51%   Tabs &
        Journals

Adonai alone is our portion. He satisfies us fully and completely. We don't yearn for the things of the past. We are not desperate for friends. We don't have to indulge in frivolous spending on unnecessary items. I used to spend money and shop all the time. I owned more than enough clothing and material things and was still lost. I learned that all the material things in the world still couldn't satisfy me. It only masked the real me. God knows what we need and when we need it. He is an omniscient being who knows all things and Jehovah Shammar, who is always there.

As children of the Father who is in heaven, we inherit, by virtue of our joint heirship with Jesus, all the riches of the covenant of grace; and the portion which falls to us sets upon our table the bread of heaven and the new wine of the kingdom. Ask Yahweh Nissi to fill your cup every morning. The Lord provides everything you will need to get through your day. He gives us all the strength needed to speak like Him, act like Him, and respond to situations like He does.

We do not have to wait until we get to heaven to experience God's banquet house. His overflowing grace is something we experience as Christians in this life.

Jesus said, "I came that they might have life, and might have it abundantly" (John 10:10b). That is a cup running over with God's grace. He does not just give us the gift of eternal life when we first believed, but He keeps on giving eternal life. Jesus gives us Himself (John 14:6). He is this abundant life. It is God's kind of life. "My cup overflows," means it is not just full; it is "running over,' filled to the brim and overflowing.

The woman of Samaria met Jesus at Jacob's well on a hot day. Jesus did not have a rope and a bucket to draw the water from the well so He asked the woman for a drink of water to quench His thirst. In the course of the conversation with the woman Jesus said, "If you knew the gift of God, and who it is who says to you, 'Give Me a drink, you would have asked Him, and He would have given you living water'" (John 4:10).

Jesus was ready to give this woman, who was a slave to sin, running water. "Whoever drinks of the water that I shall give him shall never thirst; but the water that I shall give him shall become in him a well of water springing up to eternal life" (v. 14).

Jesus a few chapters later tells us, "If any man is thirsty, let Him come to Me and drink. He who believes in Me, as the Scriptures said, 'from his innermost being shall flow rivers of living water" (John 7:37-38). These are rivers from the depths of one's being. Jesus did not say just a trickle now and then, but rivers gushing forth from within you. In the next verse Jesus tells us this is the work of the Holy Spirit.

God has made every provision for the believer to live a life that overflows with God's grace. The Holy Spirit baptized every true believer into the body of Christ the moment he first believed on Christ as his Savior. We receive one baptism, but many fillings of the Holy Spirit. God's desire is that we be continually under the control of His Spirit.

My cup runs over because He "is able to do exceedingly abundantly beyond all that we ask or think, according to the power that works within us." That is the believer who has received the fullness of God, and grace upon grace. It is the superabundance of life that we receive through the Spirit in Christ Jesus. This is the fullness of life Jesus gives and it causes our cups to run over with the fullness of joy. We should want to be so flooded with God's love that it will overflow into our relationship with Him, with ourselves, and others.

A great principle of the Christian life is the more you receive, the more you want. If your cup is overflowing, you want more of Him, and the wonderful thing is it will never run dry. All you have to do is come and drink. This super abounding life in Christ is ever growing, expanding and increasing as we are "changed from Glory into Glory" (2 Cor. 3:18). Our cup overflows by drinking a life that changes us "from glory to glory."

Receive God's healing and allow the Spirit of God to have his way in your heart. Our Father will fill you with all the reassurance that you need to have a joyful, fulfilled life. Lift your hands toward heaven and say:

"Fill my cup Lord, I lift it up Lord. Come fill this thirsting in my soul. Bread from Heaven feed me until I want no more. Fill my cup, fill it up and make me whole."

Gaining Momentum

As your cup overflows with God's love, don't look back. You are gaining strength now to move forward with your life. Let the past stay in the past and walk in your deliverance. It is imperative to maintain your deliverance from what you have done and what someone has done to you.

Remember the scriptures in Isaiah state that Jesus came to heal the brokenhearted, bind our wounds, and heal our bruises. He came to give us the oil of joy. Immerse yourself in it from the top of your head to the souls of your feet. Put on a garment of praise instead of heaviness and beauty instead of ashes. Shout because God has released you from captivity and has recovered your sight. You can see clearly where you are going. You have a brand new direction, perspective, and purpose. No longer are you downtrodden and distressed or oppressed. You are not damaged goods, not broken or destroyed, Hallelujah!

God is with you right now. He has brought you to the end of a painful season in your life. I encourage you to be all that God has created you to be. Be determined, faithful, and committed to our Lord and Savior. Purpose to communicate with the heavenly Father every day because you are going to need Him all the time. Paul's prayer in Ephesians 3:16-19 says "*I pray that out of his glorious riches he may strengthen you with power through his Spirit in your inner being, so that Christ may dwell in your hearts through faith. And I pray that you, being rooted and established in love, 18 may have power, together with all the Lord's holy people, to grasp how wide and long and high and deep is the love of Christ, 19 and to know this love that surpasses knowledge—that you may be filled to the measure of all the fullness of God.*

The inner being is where your emotional healing takes place. Satan wants to keep that part of you wounded. He wants to keep you broken inside so that when other trials come your way, you can't handle it. But the devil is a liar! God's Holy Spirit dwells within you and in your heart. The Holy Spirit will strengthen and reinforce His mighty power. The Lord will sustain you and never let you fall (Psalm 55:22).

When we are strengthened internally as well as externally, we can deal with other circumstance of life that will come our way.

Press on to your victory: *Philippians 3:12*

Not that I have already obtained all this, or have already arrived at my goal, but I press on to take hold of that for which Christ Jesus took hold of me. 13 Brothers and sisters, I do not consider myself yet to have taken hold of it. But one thing I do: Forgetting what is behind and straining toward what is ahead, 14 I press on toward the goal to win the prize for which God has called me heavenward in Christ Jesus.

14

God Rewards Faithfulness

"At some point in life the world's beauty becomes enough. You don't need to photograph, paint, or even remember it. It is enough." Toni Morrison

No matter how much you have gone through and how rough times have been, God rewards those who stick close by Him. If you are like me, you may have fallen into a few traps and temptations along the journey, but God! He is able to keep you from falling. The Lord does that for His faithful and committed children of God. In Hebrews 11:6 the Bible says, *"But without faith it is impossible to please Him. For he that cometh to God must believe that He is, and that He is a rewarder of those who diligently seek Him."*

It is important to realize that God Almighty is a loving Father, and He can take care of us better than we can take care of ourselves. When we are faithful to Him, he brings goodness to us. My life was a mess, yet I still called on the name of Jesus through it. I didn't really know how to serve God with all my heart at that time and He knew it. But as long as I tried, the Lord stuck with me. I know the Lord stayed with me because, He said in His Word, *"Be strong and courageous. Do not be afraid or terrified because of them, for the LORD your God goes with you; he will never leave you nor forsake you."* Deuteronomy 31:6

I couldn't see my way out for a long time, but as I persevered with God one step at a time, He sent special rewards and blessings my way. Our Father sent blessings my way for doing the right thing and doing it His way. That motivated me to keep on striving to transform from the old me to the new person in Christ Jesus. God's very character and nature is to show love to those who diligently (constantly, persistently, conscientiously) seek him.

God wants us to expect a reward. He wants to give you double for your trouble. Believe for and look forward to your reward. Believe that He wants to bless not punish. So don't dwell in the past or on what you have been through. Set your sight on what God is doing as you are building your life with Him. Our hope is built on nothing less, than Jesus blood and righteousness. Christ endured on the cross because he desired the prize on the other side. We too are to continue on our journey with patience and tenacity, looking to the author and finisher of our faith.

I also want to encourage you to be strengthened in the Lord because trials and tribulations will come your way. We all will go through testing and no one is exempt from them. They come many times when you least expect it. Your morning starts off great and before the day is over, chaos kicks in. As long as you are pursuing God, the enemy will be on your heels waiting for you to fall. Always be ready and prepared with a response. Prayer and staying close to God is essential in your life at this point. Take everything to God in prayer.

Do not fear and trust God (*2 Timothy 1:7 For God hath not given us the spirit of fear, but of power and of love and of a sound mind.*) Don't stop serving the Lord because problems come. This is the best time to commit to God in the difficult times. When the devil sees that he is not affecting your walk with God, he will leave you alone, at least until he comes back with another scheme.

Scripture says in Galatians 6:9 *And let us not be weary in well doing, for in due season we shall reap, if we faint not.*

Critical steps to take when problems arise:

1. Stay emotionally stable
2. Trust God
3. Pray immediately to avoid fear
4. Keep serving the Lord
5. Expect your reward

These steps should be practiced even when you are not having trials as well. Don't wait for the storm to come and you don't have a plan in place.

Enjoy God's Favor

Just as Jesus was humble when He hung on the cross, I encourage you to stay humble in your victory. You didn't do it by yourself; it was only by the grace and favor of God that you are still here. Continue to speak into your life by confessing, "I have the favor of God, I live in the favor of God, I walk in the favor God." Call those things that are not as though they are and they will manifest in your life.

When those blessings come, enjoy them. For those who have been through abuse, learn to shake the dust off and enjoy the free gift of God's grace.

The more you are humble, the more you will enjoy God's favor in your life. Greater grace requires greater humility. *1 Peter 5:5 All of you, clothe yourselves with humility toward one another, because, "God opposes the proud but shows favor to the humble."* Humility finds favor with God and man. Because of their trustworthy temperament, the spirit of the humble solicits trust and blessings.

Like honey attracts a bee, so the Lord's heart is drawn to the humble. It is a sweet exchange when the Holy Spirit fills a submissive soul.

Never forget where He's brought you from and where He wants to take you. Your humble heart, in the eyes of the Lord, prepares you for His blessings.

As you are basking in the new joys of life, don't get so caught up that you don't share your testimony. There are many people, men and women, who need to hear your story. They yearn for transformation and deliverance, but don't know how to come out. You are now in position to be used of God just like me. I tell my story because what seemed impossible became possible through Christ Jesus.

I have to tell them they can be free. You can let go of the past. You can live a fulfilled, healthy, and stable life. I have to tell them, "Oh! Taste and see that the Lord is good!" El Shaddai is sweeter than the honey comb. You are the Redeemed of the Lord. His banner over you is love, the Ancient of Days watches over you, and made you free! Romans 8:1-2 *There is therefore, no condemnation to those who are in Christ Jesus, because the law of the Spirit who gives life has set you free from the law of sin and death.*

You must declare and maintain the reality that you are an overcomer and more than a conqueror. If God be for you, who can be against you? It is God who justifies. Declare and decree that nothing shall separate you from the love of God: Romans 8:38-39 *I am convinced that neither death nor life, neither angels nor demons, neither the present nor the future, nor any powers, 39 neither height nor depth, nor anything else in all creation, will be able to separate us from the love of God that is in Christ Jesus our Lord.*

Habakkuk 3:18 *yet I will rejoice in the Lord, I will be joyful in God my Savior.* Go forth in the Lord and in the power of His might. No weapon formed against you shall prosper. Don't be afraid, but be encouraged. *Keep the Book of the Law always on your lips; meditate on it day and night, so that you may be careful to do everything written in it. Then you will be prosperous and successful* (Joshua 1:8). This is your season for breakthroughs and supernatural manifestations. If you will believe and receive it, it's yours.

15

Spiritual Therapy for Victory

"Thou shalt also decree a thing and it shall be established unto thee: and the light shall shine upon thy ways." Job 22:28.

Once you make a decree, heaven has to ensure that it comes to pass and what you don't have heaven must provide it for you. Proverbs 18:20 says. "A man's belly shall be satisfied with the fruit of his mouth; and with the increase of his lips shall he be filled." From this day forward watch what you say.

Self-defeating words affect your destiny and bring death. Do not verbalize your complaints; they can alter your destiny. Today command success into your day by speaking and decreeing: life, success, prosperity, health, wealth, greatness, love, repentance, joy, peace, salvation, and wholeness into your life. Change the direction of your life by praying the prayer of victory and making declarations over your life:

Father God, thank you for miraculous healings, supernatural blessings, and for covering me all this time. Your love is as strong as death, and every sin. I know the weapons of my warfare are not carnal, but they are mighty through God, to the pulling down strongholds. Therefore, I pull down every stronghold that has delayed and hindered the promise of God in my life (2 Corinthians 10:4). I take authority of every evil spirit and command it to get out of my environment. Lord contend with those who contend with me and fight against those who fight against me. (Isaiah 49:25). Teach my hands to war and my finger to fight (Psalms 144:1). Lord you are my shield and buckler, stand up for me! Lord secure my feet; give me hinds feet to stand in my high places (Psalms 18:33). Lord disintegrate the plots and plans of the enemy. I replace every ill spoken word with the Word of the Lord concerning my life, ministry, family, friends, and business.

Today, I walk in the timing of the Lord. Every blessing with my name on it comes to me with no delay. I decree and declare that my set time of favor with man and God is now! This is the year of God's great manifestations.

In Jesus' name, Amen.

16

Daily Bread for Maintaining your Deliverance

Journal and Workbook

"Plan your hours to be productive...Plan your weeks to be educational...Plan your years to be purposeful. Plan your life to be an experience of growth. Plan to change. Plan to grow." Iyanla Vanzant

This final chapter includes daily bread for your spiritual growth and encouragement. It has been designed for you to take twenty to thirty minutes a day to reflect on God's Word. The spiritual benefits of reading and journaling will be well worth the investment of your time. It is also purposed to incorporate consistent spiritual disciplines for maintaining your deliverance.

Allow this chapter to educate, equip, encourage, and empower your spirit.

Write Ephesians 6:10-13

_____

_____

_____

Chapter 1: Our Inner Life with God

1. Through seeking God and reading His Word, the Lord's main concern is our _____ _____, because that is where we enjoy His presence.
2. Write Luke 17:21
3. Write 2 Corinthians 2:14
4. God is the champion at bringing people from a place of _____ to a place of _____ _____.
5. Write Psalm 118:17
6. If God's kingdom rules within us, we will enjoy _____, _____, and _____ in the Holy Spirit.
7. Write Hebrews 13:6

Daily Bread Isaiah 61:1-4

🕮 The Holy Spirit is here to preach good news to people who have been hurt.

🕮 To bind up your wounds and heal your hurts and broken hearts.

🕮 To declare liberty to the captives.

   A. Physical (mental, emotional, and the will)
   B. Spiritual

Chapter 2: Residue of Abuse

1. What is the definition of abuse?

   _____

   _____

2. What are some of the forms of abuse?

   _____

   _____

3. God created us for _____ and _____.
4. To be healed of pain and abuse, you must _____ to get well.
5. Read Mark 5:25-28 and Mark 11:22-24
6. Jesus wants to open the prison and the eyes of those who are bound. Remember you must walk out.

Daily Bread for Maintaining your Deliverance

Are you an "emotional prisoner"? If so, how long have you been in that condition?

_____

_____

7. Hurting people hurt people. Who have you hurt as a result of being hurt?

_____

_____

Daily Bread

📖 To proclaim the acceptable year of the Lord.
  A. Matthew 11:2-6–Jesus is the only answer.
  B. Luke 4:18-19- Jesus was sent to heal and send forth as delivered.
      1. Oppressed
      2. Downtrodden
      3. Bruised
      4. Crushed

📖 Jesus will grant (give) consolation and joy to those who mourn.
  A. Consolation- To comfort or strengthen in time of grief. Consolation may be brought through God doing something special for you.

📖 He gives "beauty for ashes."

📖 Praise for depression and heaviness

📖 He makes us "trees of righteousness."
  A. Lofty
  B. Strong
  C. Magnificent

📖 He will use you to rebuild other ruined lives.
  A. The devastation of many generations.

Chapter 3: A Recurring Cycle

The cycle of abuse is spiritual bondage. Abuse being passed down from generation to generation is a generational curse. The chain must be broken.

1. Review 2 Samuel Chapter 11. What misfortune and affliction did you set in motion in your family?

   _____

   _____

2. Do you know your abuser? Did your abuser come from a dysfunctional background?

   _____

   _____

It's time to break the cycle.

3. Write Deuteronomy 30:15-19

   _____

   _____

4. Sin is _____ and evil leads to _____.
Read John 6:23.
5. Choose to live today because someone's _____ _____ on you.

Daily Bread: Facing Real Truths

Foundational Scriptures:
Isaiah 42:1-3–Jesus has come to reveal truth.
Isaiah 42:7- To open the eyes of the blind.
John 8:31-32–The Truth will set you free.

   A. Hidden wounds, hurts, sins, etc. can be like rotten food hidden in a refrigerator- you smell the stink but don't know where it's coming from.

   B. Are you hiding because facing the truth is too painful?

   C. Each area of liberty will require facing or seeing "a truth" that doesn't always (but may) bring pain. Are you in denial?

📖 D. When you hide behind a doorway of pain (wounded emotions), you have to come back through that same doorway to freedom.

📖 E. You can separate parts of yourself from yourself.

The Importance of Resisting "Self-Pity"

📖 A. Do you want to be pitiful or powerful?

📖 B. A <u>reason</u> to feel sorry for yourself doesn't equal the <u>right to</u> .

📖 C. II Corinthians 5:17- We are new creatures in Christ.

📖 D Philippians 3:13- One thing I do, forgetting what lies behind and pressing on to what lies ahead.

📖 E. Isaiah 43:18-19- Do not remember the former things; neither consider the things of old. Behold, I am doing a new thing! **Now** it springs forth; do you not perceive and know it and will you not give heed to it? I will even make a way in the wilderness and rivers in the desert.

📖 You can't hide from your past. Face it, but don't dwell there. Let Jesus take you by the hand and let Him lead you to "the new thing."

Chapter 4: Rotten Roots

The fruit in our lives (our behavior) comes from somewhere. A person who is violent is that way for a reason; bad behavior is like bad fruit of a bad tree with bad roots.

1. The root of behavioral addictions is;_____, coupled with _____, _____, and _____.

2. So why do unclean spirits work so hard to keep a person 'locked up/bound' concerning their failure or struggle?

_____

_____

_____

Write James 5:16

3. What is the true root of your behavioral addictions? What is your beginning that you have kept hidden?

_____

4. Bad fruit produces depression, negativism, self-pity, quick temper, and a controlling and domineering spirit.

Review: Types of Addictive Behavior
   More people are "out of control" than "in control"
   A. Alcohol, drugs
   B. Food- Obesity; sixty percent of women and fifty percent of men are overweight.
   C. Feeling Addictions
      1. Rage, anger, fear, hostility, excitement- For example a **Joy** addict wears a constant frozen smile. They are never angry, laugh at inappropriate times, and only speak of happy things.
   D. Thought Addictions
      1. Worrying- Nonstop talking
      2. Lustful thoughts
      3. Deception
      4. Rebellion
   E. Will Addictions
      1. Manipulate – I want what I want, when I want it. Self-centered and have to have their own way.
      2. Controlling- He can no longer submit the things he wants to logic or reason. He must have his own way.
      3. Sex
      4. Money
   F. Too Passive- An opposite extreme in people who totally give their will over to others and become passive. They feel they don't deserve anything they want.
   G. Re-enactments
      1. Many abused people re-enact their own abuse on their children or repeatedly put themselves in situations as adults that produce the same type of thing that happened to them as a child.

The Solution
   A. "The only way out is through."

1. Isaiah 43:1-2 Don't fear, you are Mine. When you go through the fire, I will be with you.
2. Hebrews 6:11 –Be diligent and sincere (all the way through), so you can realize and enjoy fullness with the Lord.
B. "Pass it back or pass it on"
1. Learn where to place blame.
2. Ephesians 6:12- Give it back (the problem and its results) to the devil where it came from. Pluck it up from the root.
C. II Corinthians 3:18- Come with an unveiled face (without excuse, desiring to see truth).
D. There are no quick fix methods to eliminate the problem of addictive behavior. But there is an answer.
Jesus said I John 14:6, "I am the Way."

Chapter 5: My World (The Beginning)

In the fifth chapter I began to share about what my mother's life was like growing up. It was necessary to get this information because it unlocked answers that were vital to my healing.

In this section of the workbook, find out as much as you can about the origin of your abuse. Write it out and begin accepting the truth.

It's time to release and talk about it.
Who abused you? _____
How long? _____
Describe the abuse. _____
_____
_____

Is your offender a person who has been abused also? How?
_____
_____

Is it generational abuse?
_____

Was there ever an apology?

Did you use abusive behavior on someone else?

Do you see an abusive pattern in your life?

    Understand that God loves you and knows all about your circumstances. He knows every detail. Our Father is so amazing in that He always leaves us with Hope. He rescues us by His love.
Write 1 John 4:18

Read Matthew 26:41
Write 2 Corinthians 5:7

    What do you believe about your relationship with God?
Do you believe that He loves you?

Read 1 John 4:16-19

When you fail, do you stop receiving God's love because you feel guilty or condemned?

The enemy's goal is to keep you from God's love, because God's love is the main factor in our emotional healing.

You and I are created for love.

Daily Bread
    Psalm 4:3 I confess I am set apart to serve God."

Chapter 6: My Damascus Road
    Have you stopped to take an overview of your life from its beginning to where you are now? I gave you a peek inside of what I was

like on a daily basis and how I treated people. God would have called my lifestyle detestable. My life resembled the Apostle Paul. Paul said he was the worst of sinners. His life changed on the Damascus Road. The Lord also saved an undeserving person like me and turned my life around. To God be the Glory for the great things He has done!

Time to Journal

Write about your character due to abuse. What are you like on a daily basis and how do you treat people? What strongholds have you allowed to operate in your life that needs to be broken? Do you hold unforgiveness? Do you have trust issues?

_____
_____
_____
_____

Do you remember the day, place or what you were doing when God really got your attention? Talk about the day that God stopped you in your tracks and told you, "enough is enough." Did you listen and obey? Did you procrastinate? What did you start doing that you were not doing before? Or are you in a stuck place and can't seem to move ahead?

_____
_____
_____

Tips to Move Ahead Spiritually

Follow the Holy Spirit
1. Allow the Holy Spirit to lead, guide, and direct you in the healing process. God has already sent Jesus Christ to come to earth and purchase your complete healing.
2. Who is the "Comforter"? _____
   _____

Write John 16:7

3. What names does Jesus call the Holy Spirit? (see the Amplified Bible version)

   _____, _____, _____

   _____, _____,

   and _____.
4. Which is your favorite name and why?

   _____

5. Don't run around looking for counsel from just anyone. God is not obligated to anoint what He did not initiate. When you are in trouble, go to the throne before you go to the phone. Pray first.
6. Only the Holy Spirit through the Word of God and His power to change can convince a shameful, abused person that he has been made righteousness through the shed blood of Jesus Christ.
7. The Holy Spirit is powerful and mighty and able to do what people can never do on their own.

Read Psalm 127:1

Daily Bread

Psalm 145:4 "I confess the gracious hand of God is on me."

Chapter 7: The Healing Process

We can be set free and no longer bound in the chains of the past. Are you ready to be free? Then allow the Lord to go into the secret place hidden in your heart that no one has ever entered. Let God in and trust Him with you (your heart, mind, and soul) so that the healing process can begin.

1. If you have been bound emotionally and spiritually for any number of years, it's going to take some time to undo _____ _____ and replace them with _____ _____.
2. Read 1 John 4:18

   Be willing to open your heart before the Lord and drop your defenses.

3. In working towards healing, put _____, ____ _____ and _____ under your feet and allow God love you.
4. Stop looking for love in all of the wrong places and things that make you feel good temporarily.
5. Accept God's love by being conscious of it and by putting your faith in it.
   Read 1John 4: 16
6. Stop expecting people to give you what only _____ can provide.
7. Let go of false sense of security through people, and trust in genuine _____ in God.
   Read Psalm 40:2

Identify five (5) tips to start your spiritual house cleaning. Give an example of each. Write examples that relate to your life.
1. _____
2. _____
3. _____
4. _____
5. _____

How to remove spiritual strongholds permanently
1. You need to replace areas of darkness and flood them with _____, _____, _____, _____, _____, _____, _____, _____, and an accountability partner.
2. When_____, choose the Word of God.
   Read Psalm 34:17-19
3. Know your position in Christ, you have_____.
   Read Matthew 16:19
4. Keep _____and don't give up. Matthew 7:7-8

Understanding Curses
What is a curse?

_____

_____

What is perversion?

_____

_____

1. Generational curses are very real, but can be broken.
Write Galatian 3:13-14 (Make it personal by placing your name in it.)
What are the four steps to break the generational curse in your life?
1. _____
2. _____
3. _____
4. _____

Daily Bread
   Matthew 5:6 "I confess I have a desire for the things of God."

Chapter 8: Finishing the Race
1. It is always much harder to finish than it is to start. There are no quick-fix methods to emotional and spiritual healing.
Read 2 Corinthians 3:18
2. Temptations will come, but purposing your life in God will keep you from falling into _____ and _____.

   Write 2 Timothy 2:26

   _____

   _____

3. Deny satan access into your life and renew _____ _____ to the things of God. Romans 12:2
4. Create a sacred dwelling place for you and God. Your alone time is spent there in His presence. Nothing unclean should enter.

Daily Bread for Maintaining your Deliverance

Read John 4:24-26
5. Stand firm in the choice to take up your cross and follow Christ. Matthew 16:24-25

_____

_____

6. Sacrifice and obedience, and Prayer and Faith becomes a lifestyle.
7. What spiritual practices will you implement in your life?
_____   _____   _____

Daily Bread
Jeremiah 29:11 "I confess my future is blessed."

Chapter 9: Exercise Patience for the Promises
Write Deuteronomy 7:22

_____

_____

1. Jesus Christ, our _____ _____, endured discomfort and irritation without complaining.
2. Every _____, _____, _____, _____, or _____, turn it over to the Lord and live.
Read Hebrews 10:22-23
3. Start looking at _____ as God giving you an opportunity to _____ your faith and patience.
4. Romans 10:11 says, "Anyone who _____ in Him (Jesus) will never be put to _____."
5. The lasting _____ are everything that you obtain through Christ Jesus.
6. The reward of patience is the Promise.
Read 2 Corinthians 1:20-22
7. Leave your old _____ up, _____ _____ and _____ spirit at the altar and pick up your eternal blessings from heaven.
8. The prerequisite of the blessings and promises is having faith.

Broken but Not Destroyed

Read Romans 4:16
Write the 7 Promises of God to Man in practical terms.
1. _____
2. _____
3. _____
4. _____
5. _____
6. _____
7. _____

Daily Bread
Psalm 37:23 "I confess my steps are ordered."

Chapter 10: Forgive Your Abusers
1. People that have been abused find it hard to _____ their abusers.
2. Do you feel right now that you still can't forgive and ask God, "Why should I forgive?"
3. The _____ of this sin destroys and eats away at your inner being.
4. What are the steps that lead to forgiving?

A._____
_____
_____

B._____
_____
_____

C._____
_____
_____

D._____

5. God is working to _____ His purpose and in the process you get the promise.
6. Forgiveness does not depend on whether or not the person being forgiven deserves it. *Forgiveness is a choice that is made as an act of obedience to God's Word.*
7. God through the power of the _____ _____ lives in you if you are born again. He alone can heal your inner man.
8. God gives us more grace to humble ourselves, put _____ aside along with _____ and _____.
   Write Matthew 5:44-45
9. What is God's instruction on forgiving in Luke 6: 27-28?
10. We must remember what Jesus Christ said on the cross, in agony and pain for things that were not his fault.
    Write Luke 23:34

What You Speak Matters

Letting go of those who have offended you means not commenting anymore on the matter.

1. Proverbs 20:19 says, "A gossip betrays a confidence; so avoid anyone who talks too much."
2. Romans 1:29 also says, "They are gossips". There are many forms of gossip and the Bible clearly says to stay away from those who do it.
3. Stop planting seeds (conversation that makes the listener question or assume something about the character of a person or group). God wants us to stop it because it is sin.

What are the strategies to help resist gossip?
A._____
B._____
C._____
4. What are the types of gossip?

5. The ways of the world seem right, but the Bible tells us in Romans 12:2 Do not _____ to the pattern of this world, but be _____ by the renewing of your _____. Then you will be able to test and approve what God's will is—his good, pleasing and perfect will.
6. If you truly forgive, resist gossip every day and speak Jesus.

Daily Bread
John 10:4 "I confess I know the voice of the Good Shepherd."

Chapter 11: Restoring Trust
Psalm 41:9 Even my close friend, someone I trusted, one who shared my bread, has turned against me.
1. There is nothing wrong with having good friends, but instead of trusting them as your _____, God Almighty has to be your only _____.
2. When you _____ to live for God, you must _____ Him completely.
Write Proverbs 3:5-6
3. Can you lay hurt, bitterness, pain, fear, and anxiety at the feet of Jesus and leave it there?
4. Trusting the Lord with every fiber of your being allows Him to restore _____, _____, and _____ in you.
5. What does Jeremiah 17:5-8 mean to you?
Will you place everything in God's hand trusting that the Lord knows what He is doing? _____

_____

_____

_____

6. In choosing to trust God with your _____, He can now restore your _____ _____: image, health, strength, stability, peace, love, patience, perseverance, gentleness and faith.
Read Jeremiah 18:6

Be Thankful
One of the steps in restoration is being thankful.
1. God's Word actually commands us to be _____.
Write Colossians 3:15

_____
_____
_____

2. What expensive gift did Christ purchase for us with His own blood?
3. Know that God is a great God and has your _____ _____ in mind.

Scripture Meditation:
1 Thessalonians 5:18 Give thanks in all circumstances; for this is the will of God in Christ Jesus for you.

Daily Bread
John 10:4 "I confess I know the voice of the Good Shepherd."

Chapter 12: Fill My Cup
Psalm 16:5 Lord, you alone are my portion and my cup; you make my lot secure.

Confessions:
- I am no longer empty and rejected, but filled with God's love and strength.
- No longer am I looking for something to make me feel good.
- Adonai alone is my portion. He satisfies me fully and completely.
- I inherit, by virtue of our joint heirship with Jesus, all the riches of the covenant of grace.
- Lord, fill my cup every morning. I know you will provide everything I need to get through the day.
- I am overflowing with rivers of living water that will never run dry. I have eternal life through Christ Jesus.

📖 Father God is able to do exceedingly abundantly beyond all that we ask or think, according to the power that works within us.

📖 I receive God's healing and allow the Spirit of God to have his way in my heart.

Gaining Momentum

You are gaining strength now to move forward with your life.

1. It is imperative to maintain your deliverance from what you have done and what someone has done to you.
2. Jesus came to heal the brokenhearted, bind our wounds, and heal our bruises.
Isaiah 61:1-3
3. Put on a garment of _____ instead of _____ and beauty instead of ashes. Shout because God has _____ you from captivity and has recovered your _____. You can see clearly where you are going. You have a brand new _____, _____, and _____. No longer are you _____ and distressed or oppressed. You are not damaged goods, not _____ or _____.
Read Ephesians 3:16-19
4. The Holy Spirit will strengthen and reinforce His mighty power. The Lord will sustain you and never let you fall (Psalm 55:22).
Write Philippians 3:13-14

_____

_____

_____

_____

Daily Bread

📖 Matthew 16:21 For where your treasure is, there will your heart be also.

Chapter 13: God Rewards Faithfulness

Galatians 6:9 And let us not be weary in well doing, for in due season we shall reap, if we faint not.

Write Hebrews 11:6

_____

_____

2. When we are _____ to Him, he brings goodness to us.
3. Do you believe that the Lord is with you wherever you go? Explain.
4. God's very character and nature is to show love to those who _____ (constantly, persistently, conscientiously) seek him.
5. Our _____ is built on nothing less, than Jesus blood and righteousness.
6. The enemy will be waiting for you to fall. Always be _____ and _____ with a response. Prayer and staying close to God is _____ in your life at this point.
   Read 2 Timothy 1:7
7. What are the critical steps to implement when problems arise?
   A._____
   B._____
   C._____
   D._____
   E._____
8. Speak into your life by confessing, "I _____ the favor of God, I _____ in the favor of God, I _____ in the favor God."
9. Greater _____ requires greater humility. 1 Peter 5:5 All of you, clothe yourselves with _____ toward one another, because, "God opposes the proud but shows favor to the humble."
10. It is a sweet_____ when the Holy Spirit fills a submissive soul.
11. As you are basking in the new joys of life, don't get so caught up that you don't share your testimony.
    Write Romans 8:1-2

_____

_____

_____

12. Maintain the _____ that you are an overcomer and more than a conqueror. If God be for you, who can be against you?

    Write 3 declarations to maintain and seal your break through.

_____

_____

Lamentations 3:22-26
Because of the Lord's great love we are not consumed,
   for his compassions never fail.
23 They are new every morning;
   great is your faithfulness.
24 I say to myself, "The Lord is my portion;
   therefore I will wait for him."
25 The Lord is good to those whose hope is in him,
   to the one who seeks him;
26 it is good to wait quietly
   for the salvation of the Lord.

Habakkuk 3:18 yet I will rejoice in the Lord, I will be joyful in God my Savior.

The Lord is my light and my salvation—
   whom shall I fear?
The Lord is the stronghold of my life—
   of whom shall I be afraid?
2 When the wicked advance against me
   to devour me,
it is my enemies and my foes
   who will stumble and fall.
3 Though an army besiege me,
   my heart will not fear;
though war break out against me,

even then I will be confident.

Daily Bread

Psalm 27:1-3 The Lord is my light and my salvation; whom shall I fear? the Lord is the strength of my life; of whom shall I be afraid?

Personal Development through Prayer
"Living on Purpose"

Your Relationship with God

Examine yourself to see if you have any unconfessed sin in your life or any sinful attitudes in your heart. If you do, ask God to forgive you, and to help you stop.

Ask Him to help you resist temptation, live above sin and be more victorious.

Ask Him to help you become more pure, more obedient and dependent. Ask Him to show you what He wants you to do next, for Him or someone else.

Your Relationship with Your Family

Ask God to help you earnestly love your family and do your part to live in harmony. If you're in a conflict right now, ask God to break any power Satan has in your family, and to resolve the conflict.

Ask God to help you be able to spend more time with the family, and to draw closer to each other. If your spouse or your child is being nearly impossible to deal with, ask God to help you restrain from beating, cursing, and abusing anyone. Leave the rest to God.

Your Relationship with the World, Community, Work Place, Ministry

Ask God to help you live a consistent Christian life in front of those you're around daily. Ask Him to give you an opportunity to influence others through good deeds, integrity, Godly character, and virtue. Ask for help to instinctively build relationships in order to share your relationship with God.

Ask God to help you stand up for what is right, and not be influenced by our society.

Your Health and Finances

Ask God to help you eat healthier foods, get plenty of rest, and exercise daily. Then do your part to discipline yourself and take better care of your body, you don't belong to yourself. Your body is the temple that belongs to God.

Ask God to give you good health and strength to live for Him, with the best quality of life possible. Ask God to help you have a good attitude and a sweet spirit daily.

Ask Him to help you work on getting out of debt and control your spending. Then discipline yourself to do it. Ask God to help you put Him first in every area of your life, including finances. Ask Him to help you not become a lover of money and material things. Allow Him to become Lord over your life.

"Who Am I"

I am accepted....
- John1:12 I am God's child.
- John15:15 As a disciple, I am a friend of Jesus Christ.
- Romans 6:1 I have been justified.
- 1Corinthians 6:17 I am united with the Lord, and I am one with Him in spirit.
- Colossians 2:9-10 I am complete in Christ.
- Colossians 1:13-14 I have been redeemed and forgiven of all my sins.

I am secure....
- Romans 8:11 I am free from condemnation.
- Romans 8:28 I am assured that God works for my good in all circumstances.
- Philippians 1:6 I am confident that God will complete the good work He started in me.
- 2 Timothy 1:7 I have not been given the spirit of fear but of power, love and a sound mind.

- 2 Corinthians 1:21-22 I have been established, anointed, and sealed by God.
- 1 John 5:18 I am born of God and the evil one cannot touch me.

I am significant....
- John 15:16 I have been chosen and appointed to bear fruit.
- I Corinthians 3:16 I am God's temple.
- Ephesians 2:6 I am seated with Jesus Christ in the heavenly realm.
- Ephesians 2:10 I am God's workmanship.
- Ephesians 3:12 I may approach God with freedom and confidence.
- Philippians 4:13 I can do all things through God who strengthens me.

"Never Again"

Never again will I confess or focus on weakness because the Word says: "The Lord is the strength of My Life" (Psalm 27:1) and "The people that know their God shall be strong and carry out great exploits." Daniel 11:32

Never again will I confess or focus on "I can't" because the Word says: "I can do all things through Christ who strengthens me." Philippians 4:13

Never again will I confess or focus on doubt and a lack of faith because the Word says: "God has dealt to each one a measure of faith." Romans 12:3

Never again will I confess or focus on fear because the Word says: "God has not given me the spirit of fear, but one of power, love, and a sound mind." 2 Timothy 1:7

Never again will I confess or focus on defeat because the Word says: "God always causes me to triumph in Jesus Christ." 2 Corinthians 2:14

Never again will I confess or focus on lack of wisdom because the Word says: "Christ Jesus has become for me wisdom from God." (1 Corinthians 1:30) and "if any of you lacks wisdom, he should ask God, who gives generously to all without finding fault, and it will be given to him." (James 1:5)

Never again will I confess or focus on worries and frustration because the Word says: I am "Casting all my cares upon Him who cares for me." 1 Peter 5:7

Affirmation of Faith and Holiness

I declare and decree this day that I have been chosen, predestined according to God's plan through Christ Jesus.

I come to you Father, God with a humble heart offering all my gifts and talents you have birthed inside this vessel.

I am in awe to serve the body of Christ and humanity according to your will Lord so that I can be used as a living sacrifice for your Kingdom and Glory.

Lord, as I examine my heart and look into the mirror seeking a deeper understanding from the Holy Spirit with my calling, please make it reflect you more and more.

Father God, purify my soul and my motives, endow me with the patience to wait on you Lord. Allow me to sing, dance, pray, and intercede on behalf of others.

Father God, help me to purpose to be better than yesterday every day as I promise to live you Jesus on the inside.

Anoint me Lord this day with a double portion of Elijah's spirit and keep my vessel whole.

Help me to speak exactly what you would have me to speak as I surrender my will and my way back to you. Help me to live a life of Integrity, Virtue, and Godly character.

Lord, help me as your servant to encourage and empower others. As you abide in me, help me to tread on serpents and break up fallow ground in desolate places that your name may be glorified.

Lord, help me to accept every assignment with great joy. Though I may be tempted to complain, I will keep the enemy under my feet.

Help me to remember that I have been called for your purpose, not my own.

Jesus as you sit on the right hand of the Father interceding on my behalf, allow me to usher into your throne room, usher into your anointing, and usher into the Glory of worship.

This is the year of God's great manifestation. Allow your spirit to stay connected to God's grace. Amen!

About the Author

Pastor Mavis Morisseau is the first African American woman to carry the Torah in a Messianic synagogue in the United States. She is the Founder of True Worship Prophetic Ministry Church without walls. The Lord blessed Pastor Mavis to establish Bethel House of God Prayer Line in 2011. It was later renamed True Worship Prophetic Ministry Prayer Line after her pilgrimage to Israel in 2012.

Pastor Mavis' initiatives include educating and training. She received her Masters of Creative Movement from Columbia College Chicago. She adores the Lord. Her ministry is dedicated to the total praise of Jesus Christ through apostolic leadership and discipleship. Pastor Mavis believes in activism for the disadvantaged, liberty, for the spiritually bound and healing for the broken-hearted.

Pastor Mavis works side by side with her Executive Director, Rev. Stephanie Harley. Over 15 years plus, Pastor Mavis has given of herself in the Ministry of Dance and teaching the Word of God (from Cheyenne, Wyoming, Clovis, New Mexico, Texas, Israel, Egypt, Africa, St. Marten, Costa Rica, Canada, Czechoslovakia, Rothenberg, Munich, Garmisch (Edelweiss Lodge and Resort), Germany, Trinidad, Tobago, Kingston, Jamaica, Paris, France, Austria and Vatican Rome, Italy, Okinawa, Japan, and Spain, and so many more). The Glory of heaven above, the Shekinah Glory is manifested as souls are saved, delivered, and set free as the Anointing of the Lord flows through her.

In October 2013, Pastor Mavis became a graduate of Eagles International Intercessory Prayer Institute Year Two under Eagle Karen L. Gardner out of Anchorage, Alaska. She received a Bachelor of Science Degree at the University of Maryland. Also, Pastor Mavis received her Master of Divinity at Eastern Theological Seminary in Lynchburg, Virginia.

Pastor Mavis is currently working on a Doctorate Degree in Christian Counseling. She continues to cross boundaries in the spirit realm, overcoming denominational traditions. Pastor Mavis also was blessed to minister in dance at the Senate's exquisite Rotunda in Washington DC. Her prayer, if God is willing, is to bless the First Family, President Barak Obama and family, through the Prophetic Ministry of Dance during his tenure in office. May God be magnified in all the earth!

"Purpose to be better than yesterday every day,
and promise to live Jesus on the
inside. Fall in love with Him and I promise you He will love you back."
Pastor Mavis E. Morisseau
&
Dr. Mateen A. Diop

About the Author

Thy Word, Oh Lord, is a lamp unto my feet and light unto my path. Psalm 119:105

Many people in our world today have been abused in some way and for various reasons have not been healed and restored from its affect. Statistics report that almost one in five women has been raped. Sharing their abusive experience rarely happens because of the shame, guilt, self-blame, or embarrassment they may harbor on the inside.

Pastor Mavis Morisseau has a story of her own to share of how God delivered her victoriously through the wilderness. The many trials and challenges, heart-aches and pain, strongholds and bondages, labels and stigmas that come with traumatic experiences can be overwhelming to handle alone. You don't have to walk alone.

God has a plan. Isaiah 61 says the Lord came to heal the broken-hearted, those who were crushed, emotionally wounded, and bruised.

Today Pastor Mavis is living victoriously and oversees a global ministry of Prayer and Intercession. Her God-given ministry focuses on bringing emotional healing and spiritual growth by *educating, empowering, encouraging,* and *equipping* (through the Word of God) others like herself. Following the reading, a workbook designed for reflection, encouragement, and healing for the reader is available.

You will learn:
- *Abusive behavior and the affects*
- *Breaking the curse in your life.*
- *Steps to healing and victory*
- *Maintain your deliverance and enjoy God's blessings*

Pastor Mavis Morisseau suffered many years from the effect of abuse. God has restored her mind, body, and soul for His glory. She was broken but not destroyed, and she lives to tell about it.

CPSIA information can be obtained
at www.ICGtesting.com
Printed in the USA
FFOW02n1844030415
12363FF

9 781498 429344